DEVELOPMENT OF HOTELS & RESORTS

A Project Management Based Approach

DEVELOPMENT OF
HOTELS & RESORTS

A Project Management Based Approach

S. G. Krishna Murthy

KHANNA BOOK PUBLISHING CO. (P) LTD.

Publisher of Engineering and Computer Books

4C/4344, Ansari Road, Darya Ganj, New Delhi-110002

Phone : 011-23244447-48 **Mobile:** +91-9910909320

E-mail : contact@khannabooks.com

Website: www.khannabooks.com

Dear Readers,

To prevent the piracy, this book is secured with HIGH SECURITY HOLOGRAM on the front title cover. In case you don't find the hologram on the front cover title, please write us to at contact@khannabooks.com or whatsapp us at +91-99109 09320 and avail special gift voucher for yourself.

Specimen of Hologram on front Cover title:

Moreover, there is a SPECIAL DISCOUNT COUPON for you with EVERY HOLOGRAM.

How to avail this SPECIAL DISCOUNT:

Step 1: Scratch the hologram
Step 2: Under the scratch area, your "coupon code" is available
Step 3: Logon to www.khannabooks.com
Step 4: Use your "coupon code" in the shopping cart and get your copy at a special discount
Step 5: Enjoy your reading!

Thanks,
Khanna Publishing House

Development of Hotels & Resorts
by **S. G. Krishna Murthy**

ISBN: 978-93-55380-90-6

First Edition: 2023
Reprint: 2025, 2026

To view complete list of books, please scan the QR Code:

Published by:
Khanna Book Publishing Co. (P) Ltd.
CIN: U22110DL1998PTC095547

Visit us at: www.khannabooks.com
Write us at: contact@khannabooks.com

Printed in India.

|| आ नो भद्राः क्रतवो यन्तु विश्वतः ||

(Let noble thoughts come to us from all parts of the world)

PREFACE

Hotels and Resorts, as generally understood, originated from the West. We had only "choultries" and "serais" in the past. The origin of hotels in the West is because of the industrial revolution and growth in infrastructure on a large scale, such as highways, railroads, airways, ports and harbors. Consequently, there was the development of trade, commerce, and urbanization on a large scale. Eating houses and rest houses became common, and eventually, hotels and resorts. The advancement in trade and commerce, in turn, necessitated convention centers where thousands would gather for national or international conferences on science and technology, art and literature as well as trade. Thus, hotels and resorts are now the mainstay of travel and tourism.

There are several leading hoteliers like Carlsons (Radisson), Hilton, Ritz Carlton, Marriott, Hyatt, Bethesda, Best Western, Jing Jang International, Wyndham Worldwide, ACCOR, Novotel Sofitel, Oberoi, Trident, etc. many of whom own these hotels. In addition, they manage hotel properties belonging to others worldwide.

State-run ITDC started its own venture with Hotel Asoka, the Jan Path, Akbar in Delhi, and later in other cities like Bangalore, Chennai, Lucknow, Kanpur, etc. But, they had to close down by the end of the 1990s due to mismanagement and widespread corruption. Only Hotel Asoka in Delhi, ITDC mascot have remained untouched. However, the growth of the hotel industry in India has been sluggish. Even after attaining its independence from the British, the subsequent partition, incursions by China and Pakistan and the slow economy for nearly half a century were detrimental to India. In 1990, i.e., 43 years after attaining freedom, India found itself with only one billion US dollars foreign exchange and had to pledge gold in the Bank of England to buy badly needed foreign exchange. Providentially, the government of the then Prime Minister Sri. P V Narasimha Rao threw open the economy in 1991 to global markets and successive governments had no option but to follow suit. There were hardly about 30 5-Star Hotels in the country in 1990. The Government of the then Prime Minister Sri Atal Bihari Vajpayee under took massive infrastructure projects adding highways, railroads, waterways, airports, etc. As a result, there has been an addition of over one lakh km of highways and we now have sixty fully functional airports with another 100 planned for completion in the next five years. Indian economy became the fastest growing economy in the world in 2015. We are now poised to take advantage of the fourth industrial revolution where linear growth has given way to exponential growth; scarcities have given way to abundance. India also has the advantage of demographic dividend, with 65% of its population in the age group 25 to 35, of approximately 800 million.

We now have an estimated 1,30,000 branded hotel rooms in the country at Bangalore, Mumbai, Hyderabad, Jaipur, Agra, Delhi, with world-class Hotels such as Taj West End, Ritz Carlton in Bangalore, Taj Mahal Hotel, Four Seasons and Grand Hyatt in Mumbai, Falaknuma Palace Hotel in Hyderabad, Lake Palace Hotel, Uday Vilas in Udaipur, Umaid Bhavan Palace Hotel in Jodhpur, Rambagh Palace Hotel and Hotel Raj Vilas in Jaipur, Mughal Sheraton in Delhi, Hotel Amar Vilas in Agra, etc.

As per the latest census, inland tourism has touched 2.8 billion per year, with two million foreign tourists. The revenue from tourism and hospitality currently estimated at USD 250 billion is expected to touch USD 750 billion by 2025. The country expects a GDP growth of INR five trillion by 2025. Thus the prospects for hotels and resorts look most promising. I feel this book on project management of hotel and resorts will be an excellent value-add to help budding entrepreneurs and startups in the hospitality industry.

I have given comprehensive information on what constitutes feasibility study, field studies, the role of the architects, structural engineers, interior designers, mechanical, electrical and plumbing engineers, landscape architects, signage and graphics, illumination, building automation, etc. I have given detailed suggestions for space analysis for 5-star hotels, costing details, F. F. & E. (furniture, fixtures or other equipment) differentiation, etc. I wish to tell the reader that some of the systems, standards and norms mentioned in the book are followed by leading hoteliers, architects and interior designers across the world and what I have come across in my travels in South Asia, the Far East, Europe, and America. I have drawn upon my experiences of my prolonged stay sometimes in 5-star hotels in Mumbai, Delhi, Kolkata, Kathmandu, Chennai, Colombo, Singapore, Jakarta, Bali, and Hong Kong spread over 50 years. It is my humble attempt to present all this to you in a concise format. I duly admit that the information and learning shared here are borrowed, and I have no claims of ownership over them.

About achieving revenue of USD 750 billion by 2025 and USD 1.5 trillion by 2030, we must set to work on this goal in right earnest because by developing luxury hotels and resorts in the 5-star category all along the coast from Gujarat to West Bengal, we will be exploiting sun and sand with the help of advanced expertise available to us. As architects, engineers, hoteliers, we can achieve our objective on similar lines. Despite being a small island, the tropical island of Bali in Indonesia attained revenue of USD 42 billion in 2019.

As explained in the book, ministries of tourism at Union and State Governments of India have a significant role in promoting tourism through eco-resorts. It is my humble request to them to consider the proposals and implement them to develop tourism and allied industries.

This book is primarily intended to help students of hotel management programs and startups. I hope the study of the book will significantly help hoteliers and hotel management aspirants in the development of hotels and resorts from a technical perspective.

26-10-2020 - S. G. Krishna Murthy

Vijayadashami

FOREWORD

Mr. S. G. Krishna Murthy has lifetime experience managing the construction of many hotels and resorts in India and abroad. I had the privilege of working with him on a few projects and have known him for several years. His thought processes, keen observation of facts and events have made him write this book for students of project management and young professionals.

This book deals with all the aspects of the development of hotels and resorts right from the feasibility of location, to the complete process of appointment of various professionals like architects, structural consultants, interior designers, MEP consultants, etc., coordination among the multiple teams, and also the process of design management.

Client perspectives of the role of project management have also been detailed very well.

Hotels are a service-oriented enterprise and complete coordination is essential during the design phase for finalizing the design and moving to the tendering and pre-construction phase.

In hotels, interior design and landscape play a pivotal role. Feasibility and mock-ups are vital. Furniture, fittings and equipment need to be foolproof. All these factors have been captured in this book.

Various studies like techno-commercial, field survey and their importance have been mentioned. Multiple formats for cost analysis have also been discussed.

The book will be helpful for Project Management Consultants (PMC) of hotels and resorts.

A new direction for people in power to develop the longest coast in India, spanning the nine states to be developed into clusters of resorts to attract tourists across the world and various categories, has been suggested. The establishment of a Resort Development Authority has also been recommended. Mr. Murthy has compiled all his experience in this book.

Hearty congratulations to Mr. Murthy for this book which is a ready reckoner for the development of hotels and resorts.

With best wishes,

Date: 12th January 2021

N. N. Nagendra Kumar
Resident Director, Bangalore.
Sterling Engineering Consultancy Services Pvt. Ltd.

ACKNOWLEDGEMENTS

I express my heartfelt gratitude to:

The College of Military Engineering, Kirkee (Pune) and the teaching staff of the SA-I course, based on the Royal Institute of Chartered Surveyors, U.K., in 1956. The course taught me the fundamentals of Quantity Survey, Specification and Contract Procedure in almost all engineering disciplines.

Mr. Radhe Shyam Saraf, Chairman of Saraf Group of Hotels, and his sons Mr. Arun Kumar Saraf and Mr. Umesh Kumar Saraf for giving me an opportunity to work on many of their hotel projects in Kathmandu, Delhi, Mumbai, and Kolkata as Group President/ Advisor for almost 15 years (from 1991 to 2011). This assignment enabled me to work with leading architects, interior designers, landscape and illumination consultants and project management specialists such as Louis Berger International, Wimberley Allison, Tang & Goo, Nikki & Sekkai of Japan, Arcops of Montreal, Gherzi International, Zurich, H.B.A. and Chandu Chadda Siembeda of U.S.A., Rajinder Kumar, Jasbir Sawhney, A.P. Kanvinde of Delhi.

Emily Jouzy T.D. Ltd., the U.K. for their writings about the hospitality industry and HCI MA reference book (Hotel Specific International).

Late Mr. Sitaram Chadda, co-founder of ECC (Engineering Construction Corporation), a sister concern of L&T (Larsen & Toubro), for the opportunity to work with him on his construction project, which incidentally enabled my association with the construction of the 300-room 5-star hotel, Hotel Centaur, Mumbai, India, and Yak & Yeti Hotel (Phase-I) in Kathmandu, Nepal.

Department of Atomic Energy, Trombay (Govt. of India), where I got to work closely with the famous scientists Dr. Vikram Sarabhai and Prof. M.G.K. Menon on the High Altitude Cosmic Research Project in Gulmarg, Kashmir, and other projects of the Department of Atomic Energy, Trombay. (Refer to author's profile).

Late Miss A. Mathew of Kottayam, Kerala, my senior colleague and partner at Venson International (Registered in TCDC of ESCAPE, U.N.O.), for enabling me to focus on my work with diligence, thus helping me to take up more assignments despite my advancing age.

Mr. K. V. Ramana, my son, a civil engineer, for assisting me in my work and compiling useful data for this book.

Mr. Jagadish V, my son-in-law, former Vice-President (New Projects, Bosch) for his assistance in reviewing the contents of the book and making relevant additions.

Mr. D.V. Patwardhan, retired librarian, from Bangalore, for preparing the transcription of my handwritten manuscript and reaching out to the publisher.

Padma Bhushan Shri E. Sreedharan, former Managing Director of the Delhi Metro Rail Corporation (DMRC), for his gracious words about the book, and my first granddaughter, Mrs. Janaki Venkat, for facilitating this connection.

Dr. Shruthi Prakash Venkatesh, my second granddaughter, for her invaluable assistance with editing and proofreading the drafts and liaising with the publisher on my behalf.

Mr. Mukul Seth of Khanna Book Publishing Co. (P) Ltd, for his kindness, generosity and his faith in this book that made it a reality.

Shri R. Govindarajan, my maternal uncle, who fed me and took care of my entire education. Providentially, he was there physically to congratulate me when I received my engineering degree and through most of my professional career as he lived up to 102 years. I am deeply indebted to him.

My parents, Sri. Sadahalli Gopalaiah and Smt. Alamelamma. After I graduated with a Bachelor of Science, I asked my mother if I could take up a job to help my parents overcome our family's abject poverty. My mother insisted that I complete my degree in engineering. Sadly, within a year after that, both passed away in a fortnight. It is only befitting that I dedicate this book to their memory.

Ultimately, my large and loving family for their unwavering support through my life's journey.

S. G. Krishna Murthy

PROFILE OF THE AUTHOR

Sri. S G K Murthy was born on 14th August 1926 at Sadahalli village, Bangalore Rural, Karnataka, India. He graduated in Science (B.Sc.) from Central College, Bangalore, in 1946 and completed B.E. (Civil Engineering) from B.M.S College, Bangalore, in 1951.

Awarded F.I.E. by The Institution of Engineers (India), following are some of the significant projects he was associated with:

1. Worked in M.E.S. from 1952 to 1960, Avadi Base, Chennai, Naval Armament Depot Project in Vishakapatnam, Bharat Electronics Ltd. Project, Bangalore and Armoured Static Workshops, Ahmednagar.
2. Joined Department of Atomic Energy, Govt. of India, Trombay in 1960 and worked on the following projects:
    - As Project Officer for setting up of high altitude labs for cosmic research at Gulmarg and Apharwat (Kashmir) under Mr. Vikram Sarabhai (Chairman, INCOSPAR) (Architect: Mr. A.P. Kanvinde).
    - Worked concurrently in Trombay as Executive Engineer for Department of Atomic Energy, Trombay. Job role included:
        (*a*) Planning of 400,000 sq.ft. hot laboratories for radio metallurgy, radio isotopes and radio chemistry (Consultant: Vitro International, U.S.A.)
        (*b*) Construction of Central Workshop and Stores at Trombay with Hyperbolic Shell Roof (Architect: Dr. Carbone, Italy)
        (*c*) Training in pre-stressed concrete under Mons Koveneko of STUP during 1960-61.
3. Worked as Senior Engineer at Etah Dairy Project, for Hindustan Lever Limited, Uttar Pradesh.
4. Indraprastha Thermal Power Station 182 MW, for Sikand Construction Co., New Delhi. (Consultants: Gibbs & Hill, New York)(Structural Steel & Civil Works).
5. Chief Engineer & Partner: Chadda Construction Company, Mumbai, 1969-78.
    (*a*) Slag cement project at Tatanagar and Chaibasa Cement Factory 1000 TPD. (Tons per Day) (Expansion Project of ACC).
    (*b*) Korba Alumina Project (Plant works).
    (*c*) 300 rooms 5-star Centaur Hotel, Santa Cruz Airport, Mumbai. General Construction (Architect: Mr. Willie Kaffauld, Germany. Consultants: Gherzi Eastern, Mumbai.
    (*d*) 110 Rooms, 5 Star Hotel Yak & Yeti at Katmandu on a turnkey basis for Saraf Group of Industries (H.K.). Architect: David Echeverria. Consultant: Gherzi Eastern Ltd., Mumbai.
6. Managing Director, V.S. Group of Companies, Bangalore 1978-1990.
    (*a*) KIOCL Housing Projects at Mangalore, Malleswara, Bangalore.

(*b*) Chitrapur Mutt, multi-storeyed housing and commercial project at Bangalore. Architect: K.P. Padmanabha and Zachariah and Thomas, Bangalore, respectively.

(*c*) Garment factory for LAWS (H.K.), Texan Lanka & Inter Fashion. All in Free Trade Zone, Colombo, Srilanka

(*d*) S.G.N.S.S.Group Housing at Bhilai. Architect: Zachariah and Thomas.

(*e*) Annapurna Textiles Factory at Birganj, Nepal. Consultant: Gherzi Eastern Ltd., Bombay.

(*f*) Group-I Million TPD (Tons per Day) Expansion of Yerraguntla Cement Factory for CCI, New Delhi.

7. Joined Saraf Group of Companies, Hong Kong. Worked as President (Expansion) during 1991-2001 and 2007-2010.

(*a*) 150 Rooms Hotel Yak & Yeti expansion at Kathmandu, Architect: Arcops, Montreal, Canada, K.S. Money, Chennai, India. Consultant: Gherzi Eastern Ltd., Mumbai. Interior Designer: Fiona Ennis Pty. Melbourne.

(*b*) 300 Rooms Taragaon Regency, Kathmandu, Nepal (planning only).

Architect: Nikki & Sekkai, Japan. Service Consultants: Ghazi Eastern Ltd., Mumbai.

(*c*) 400 Rooms Grand Hyatt, Vasant Kunj, New Delhi. Architect: Rajendrakumar & Associates. Structural Consultants: STUP (India).

Interior Designers: Hersch Bedner & Associates. Service Consultants: M/s. Spectral India & Mr. Deolalikar & Associates. (Also preliminaries for 900 rooms Grand Hyatt, Mumbai. Architect: Lohan Associates, U.S.A. Interior Designers: Chandu Chadda Siembeda, San Francisco, U.S.A.)

(*d*) Expansion project (350 Rooms + 100 Service Apts.) of Hyatt Regency, Calcutta. Architect: Jasbir Sawhney. Consultants: Spectral. Structural Consultants: Optimal Designs (planning only).

(*e*) Renovation of Hotel Grand, New Delhi. Interior Designer: Design Studio, U.A.E. Services: Pradhan Associates, Delhi.

(*f*) Expansion of Hotel Grand, New Delhi (Planning only).

Addition of 350 Rooms. Architect: Morphogenesis, New Delhi.

Service Consultants: Spectral, New Delhi. Interior Designers: Design Studio, U.A.E.

8. M.D., Vescons International (Regd. In ESCAP), 2001 to 2007.

(*a*) Planning of 120 Rooms Resort & Golf Course in Sikkim.

Architect: W.A.T.G. Structural Consultant: Optimal Designs

Services: Pradhan & Associates

(*b*) 2002-2007 - Planning & construction of Millennium Trade Centre at Aizawal (Hotel & Plaza).

Prime Consultants: Vescons International, Bangalore. Structural Consultant: Sterling Engineers, Bangalore. Contractors: Larson & Toubro.

(*c*) 2010-11 - Hotel Sheraton at Guwahati (planning only).

Prime Consultants & Architects: Robert Zhang, W.A.T.G., Singapore.

Service Consultants & Detailing Architects: Quadriga, Chennai.

CONTENTS

1 CHAPTER Introduction

1.1 AIMS AND OBJECTIVES OF HOTELS AND RESORTS

What are the likely hurdles in starting one? How to overcome them?

In India, Taj and Oberois are the pioneers of the Hotel industry and are also well known for their food and beverage outlets. Welcome Group started its foray into the hospitality field in the early 1980s and has some of the best hotels in the country. I spent almost twenty-five years of my career in the planning and construction of hotels. I did not come across any book that dealt elaborately with all aspects of a hospitality center or even the Project Management part of it. I thought of writing this book to help prospective entrepreneurs, students of the hospitality industry and engineers who specialize in the construction of hotels and resorts.

Man has indeed traveled a long way in search of success and fortune. The pace of travel has increased tremendously. A relatively large section of the 21st century travelers comprises business travelers in search of wealth and fame, or pleasure travelers eager to sight-see, or travelers wanting to unwind, seeking peace, sanity and time with themselves and nature. Despite conveniences bestowed by innovation and technology,there has been no escape from the stresses of daily living. Hence the increasing need for peace, relaxation and the much longed time for self and family. Hotels and resorts are an outcome of this, and they must strive to provide an environment where one can break away from the drudgery.

A resort provides holiday accommodation for tourists and holiday makers. It is the place of 'destination' unlike hotels, which are often places of transit to other destinations or places of stay during business travel. Most resorts are strategically located near lakes, mountains and hills, or seas shores with abundant scenic beauty. Based on the location and priority in the services offered, the resorts can be classified into the following categories:

- Health resorts
- Hill resorts
- Beach resorts
- Recreational resort
- Eco-resorts

The difference between hotels and resorts is, in the latter, all public areas and multi-storied guest room blocks (if any) are centralized while the guest cottages and villas are spread over a wider area. Some guest rooms are grouped as multi-layered condominiums to provide each guest room a terrace for sitting out, sunbathing, etc. Beach resorts have an added advantage with water sports such as scuba diving, snorkeling, coral reef watching, cruise access, etc. On islands like the Maldives, even the guest rooms are built on water. In hill resorts, stepped condominiums are relatively common to suit the topography. Individual cottages are avoided for security reasons. However, golf resorts in hilly areas are a big draw, like Gulmarg and Srinagar in Kashmir. In such instances, individual cottages are built on the rim of the golf course and these cottages are occupied by players and golf enthusiasts.

A resort also generally provides the following amenities similar to a hotel while the latter could be more cramped, especially the ones in big cities due to vertical growth:

- Luxury guest rooms and suites
- Banquet Halls
- High-tech gymnasium
- Spa with nature therapies
- Pool areas
- Excursions.
- Fully equipped restaurants
- Exhibition facilities
- Health and fitness centers
- Casino
- In-door and out-door games

A convention centre is a large building designed to hold a convention where individuals and groups gather, to promote and share common interests. They offer sufficient floor area to accommodate several thousand attendees. These huge buildings are fitted with the latest HVAC & audio-visual facilities, individual seating with work desks, earphones, microphones, and related communication devices. In addition, the auditorium has press boxes and access to multi-lingual translators. The central auditorium can have many annex spaces like secondary auditoriums with similar facilities for group discussions. The convention center is generally supported by a cluster of 5-star hotels or resorts with a wide selection of food and recreation facilities. E.g., Convention centers in prominent locations like Davos city, Geneva, Los Angeles, San Francisco, New York, Chicago, Kansas City, etc.

1.2 AIMS AND OBJECTIVES OF RESORTS

With people becoming increasingly environment-conscious, we see eco-friendly resorts becoming popular. The concept of eco-resorts has gained traction due to increased awareness about environmental degradation. As its name suggests, an eco-resort incorporates features and measures in its functioning where dependence on non-renewable energy sources is kept to the minimum, with maximum utilization of renewable sources of energy. Some significant guidelines followed by these resorts are:

- **Materials:** Use of easily and locally available materials for construction and furniture such as bamboo, wood, mud blocks, etc.
- **Temperature and humidity:** Maintaining the internal building conditions to reduce artificial cooling in summers and heating in winters. This is achieved by a proper study of the microclimate of the site and developing the site plans based on correct building orientation, with due consideration of factors such as sunlight, wind, etc.
- **Conservation of resources:** This includes factors like waste-water treatment, rainwater harvesting, recycling of waste, promoting the use of renewable energy sources such as solar, wind, biogas, etc., and optimizing the use of limited resources.

1.3 GENERAL

Planning, funding, and execution of hotel projects are among the most challenging jobs in construction. It wouldn't be hyperbole to call it akin to making a Bollywood movie.

Unless the box office returns of the initial days are great, one could invariably call it a flop. Likewise, unless the hotel occupation and sales at food outlets are not atleast 45 to 50% in the first year after intensive marketing in the media, reduced tariff during the prelaunch, alerting travel agents and the operators pitching in, the owner has a problem on his hands. In the hotel industry, if it does not sell today, it won't tomorrow.

Even construction has many hurdles to overcome. Sometimes, well-organized, well-funded, and well-staffed projects come to a halt without notice. It happened to one of the 5-star super deluxe projects in New Delhi I was associated with as President of the Group. The hotel plot was part of the prominent development area of the Delhi Development Authority (DDA) - about 95 acres adjoining the Nelson Mandela road in New Delhi. DDA sold it in public auction (an area of 10 acres) to the promoters, earmarked for a hotel before the auction. D.D.A. even approved the submission drawings, though there were inordinate delays. Hyatt gave their franchise for the project, and the entire design team and the operator were on board. Since the government sold the plot earmarked for hotels, we did not go for environmental clearances as the entire 95 acres plot was an approved development area. Unfortunately, there was a bombshell from the ministry of environment when we were nearly halfway through the project with the superstructure in progress. The authorities told us to halt the project as the area fell under Delhi Ridge. We had no option but to disband the project when almost Rs. 100 crores were committed. On our recourse to litigation in the apex court, the Ministry of Environment had no option but to withdraw the objections. Nevertheless, the project was delayed by almost 12 months. The promoter lost about Rs. 60 crores as expenditures in disbanding and recouping unproductive overheads and interest on borrowed money.

The Group Chairman, Mr. Radhe Shyam Saraf, wanted me to write a book on the challenges faced by entrepreneurs vis-a-vis the D.D.A.(Delhi Development Authority) and other Government agencies in New Delhi. The fact that Mr. Saraf, a soft-spoken and highly successful businessman, should have thought of "calling a spade a spade" was a culmination of several episodes involving D.D.A. and the environment ministry. I do hope the situation is much better now.

We wished to expand for the same hotel project eight years after commencement. While DDA gave the initial go-ahead and when the design team and project staff were on board, the same DDA did not approve the submission drawings for no specific reason and we had to abandon the expansion plans. Hence, it is a challenge to plan for uncertainties, and one has to take it in one's stride.

In another interesting case, there was a particular Erawan Hotel in a prominent place (PETCHABURI) of Bangkok city. The hotel is now called Grand Hyatt. There were many hurdles when Erawan Hotel was proposed to be built. At first, the roof slab collapsed, and the whole structure had to be rebuilt. Then, as the hotel was getting ready, the ship carrying plant and equipment from Europe drowned in the high seas and the management had to order the same again.

To avoid such major mishaps, someone advised the hotel owners to build a temple for Brahma (Chathurmukha) in one corner facing the main square in Petchaburi. When I visited Bangkok for the first time in 1981, I noticed the temple without any roof, with a golden image of Brahma in one corner. Four Thai dancers were dancing round the clock in front of the idol. I was astonished to hear how it came about. Moreover, I was told that the Caesar's Palace Hotel in Las Vegas had similarly put a replica of the temple.

It is a well-known fact that hotels owned by the Tatas or Welcome Group are a great success. Of course, both organizations are known to be good in funding and human resources management. They have long arms to take care of any untoward or unexpected development except for the 26/11 tragedy, which was beyond the control of management. Despite the unfortunate loss of life, including hotel staff and heavy structural damage, the hotel was back in business within a year. Therefore, question now arises as to how start-ups could survive in the face of uncertainty. While none can predict these, taking things in one's stride does help and, of course, insurance, if any. With the advancement of technology and the availability of digital services, it has been made possible for projects to progress faster, saving time and operating expenses. R.T.I. (Right to Information) has been a valuable tool, a dream in our country until a few years ago.

As is practiced today by some of the best hoteliers in the world, project management is a remarkable tool. Let us see what it is all about and how it evolved. We have the latest wonder, the Burj Khalifa in Dubai, while reaching out to the stars by sheer height, houses five to seven five-star hotels and over 3000 super deluxe apartments with several built-in malls, completed within five years.

1.4 DEFINITION OF PROJECT MANAGEMENT

Project management is planning, procurement and execution for an undertaking with a definite scope, start and finish. It is an activity in which the individual does not get directly involved but strives to maintain progress by mutual interaction and tasks of various parties, to reduce the risk of overall failures with maximum benefits and minimize costs. In other words, Project Management is the practice of initiating, planning and execution, controlling and closing the work of a team to achieve specific goals and meet sufficient success criteria at a particular time.

A project could be a temporary endeavor designed to produce a unique product or service results with a definite beginning and an end, usually time-bound, often constrained by funds or staffing.

1.5 HISTORY

Until the end of the 18th century AD, projects were generally managed by creative architects or great master builders engaged by a ruling class with a theocratic zeal or even well-to-do persons or city-states with cultural goals; or efflorescence of specific periods of history such as the Renaissance or the industrial revolution. To name a few icons: (1) Michelangelo Buonarroti, famed sculptor, painter and architect credited with St. Peter's Basilica, Sistine Chapel ceiling painting of The Last Supper - all in Rome and Statue of David in Florence, (2) architect Sir Christopher Wren who designed and supervised the St. Paul's Cathedral in London, (3) The Pharaohs of Egypt (Pyramids, Karnack, Luxor and Abu Symbol temples, (4) The Acropolis of Greece, (5) The Pallavas, Cholas and Rastrakutas (Mahabalipuram, The Brihadeshwara Temple at Tanjore, Ellora Caves, cave architecture also at Ajanta, Elephanta, etc.) and (6) Angkor Wat or Angkor of Cambodia.

From my personal experience, project management tools and techniques to complete engineering projects, with definite start and finish dates and cost, started in the middle of the 20th century in India.

Much earlier, Henry Gantt, the forefather of project management,is credited with designing the Gantt chart as a project management tool with work breakdown structures (WBS) and resource allocation.

1.6 CRITICAL PATH METHOD (CPM)

A technique to predict the project duration by analyzing the required events, a Mathematical project scheduling model was developed as a joint venture between the Du-Pont Corporation (U.S.A.) and the Remington Rand Corporation.

CPM is used for projects with deterministic activity, i.e., the time at which each activity needs to be carried out is known.

1.7 PROGRAMMED EVALUATION AND REVIEW TECHNIQUE (PERT)

The PERT was developed by the U.S. Navy in collaboration with the Lockheed Martin Corporation (manufacturers of aircraft engines) and Booz Allen Hamilton, U.S.A., as a part of the Polaris nuclear submarine project.

PERT is used where the activities to be carried out are uncertain or varied because of core differences.

Therefore CPM & PERT are used in different contexts. Regarding the methodology employed, careful consideration must be given to overall project activities, time and cost, as well as the responsibility of participants and stakeholders.

The phased approach comprises:

1. Initiation
2. Planning and Design
3. Construction
4. Monitoring and controlling
5. Completion or closing

The success of any project depends upon how well the key aspects are aligned with the contextual dynamics while approaching the project, and these are referred to as the "4 Ps":

P I Plan - Planning and forecasting activity

P II Process - Overall approach activities

P III People - Project guidance including dynamics of how they collaborate and communicate

P IV Power - Lines of authority, decision-making organigrams, power for Implementation and completion.

1.8 PROJECT MANAGEMENT IN INDIA (POST-INDEPENDENCE)

Government departments in India followed a standard schedule of rates and specifications as applicable for closing contracts, with the start and completion dates fixed, including the cost.

The Ministry of Defence followed the outlines laid down by the Royal Institute of Chartered Surveyors (U.K.) to execute works. The Bar Chart system came into being in the sixties, the CPM was followed for Hotel projects since the 70's.

In the first hotel project, I was associated with, in 1972 as the Chief Engineer and Partner for Hotel Centaur in Santa Cruz, Mumbai, we worked on bar charts. In the second hotel project, i.e., Hotel Yak and Yeti in Kathmandu in 1975-78, in addition to bar charts, we also used CPM (Critical Path Method). The CPM chart had about 950 activities in all. However, in hotel projects carried out in 1990 and beyond, we also used PERT (Programme Evaluation & Review Technique) charts.

A forward-looking economy scaffolded by technological support devoid of 'permit raj' and red tape is vital to achieving prosperity. Such a climate is absolutely essential for growth in the hospitality sector too.

2 CHAPTER
Organigram of Owner, Consultants & Project Coordinator

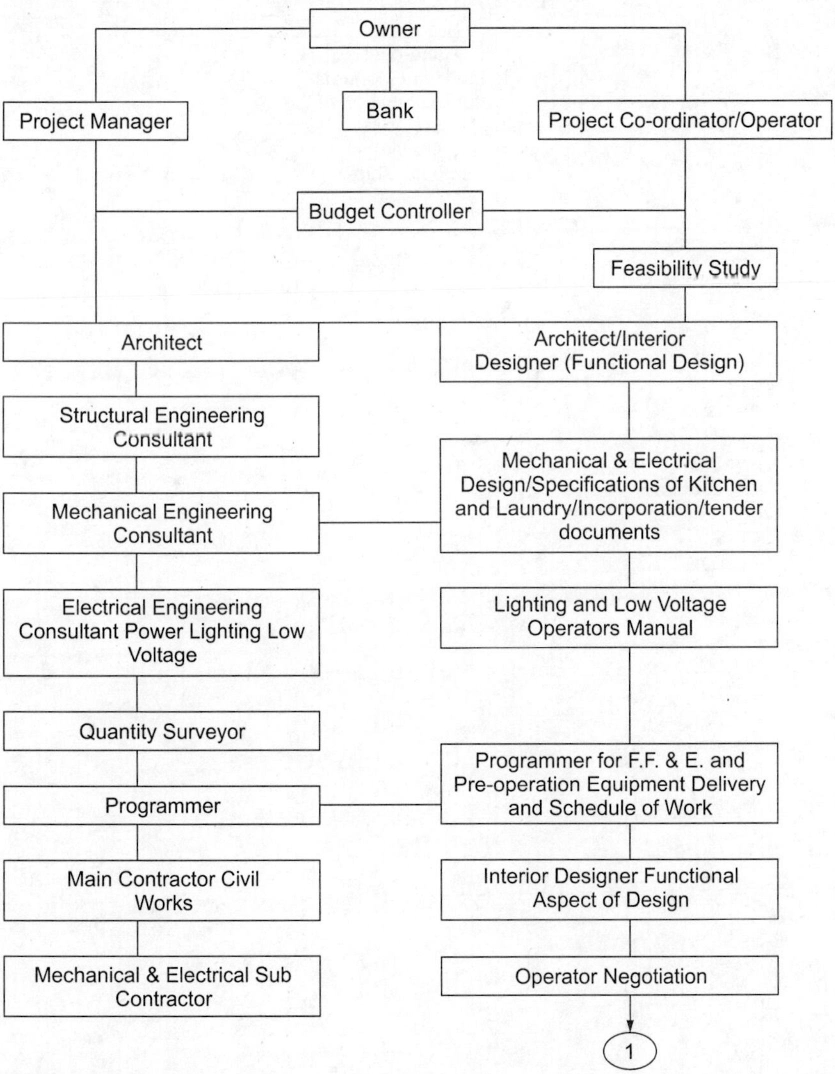

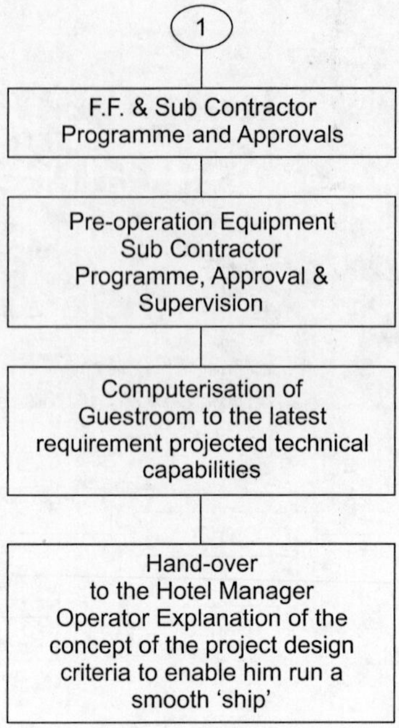
1
F.F. & Sub Contractor Programme and Approvals
Pre-operation Equipment Sub Contractor Programme, Approval & Supervision
Computerisation of Guestroom to the latest requirement projected technical capabilities
Hand-over to the Hotel Manager Operator Explanation of the concept of the project design criteria to enable him run a smooth 'ship'

CHAPTER 3 The Owner

3.1 THE OWNER

1. "Owner" could be a an individual, diploma holder in hotel management from a recognized university with at least ten years experience in the field of hospitality and who has his source of investment in the hospitality industry.
2. "Owner" could be a government or corporate body, primarily intended for the hospitality industry, to establish one more unit.
3. "Owner"could be a business house that wants to diversify into hospitality or even an airline that wants to have its hotel or resort.
4. "Owner" could be a bank that has taken over a non-performing asset like a hotel where the owners have failed in their venture and defaulted on payments to the Bank.
5. "Owner"could be a hotel chain that wants to expand its activities in a new area.

In short, the "Owner" is mostly the one who sticks his neck out to start a new venture with ambition and hope.

In all these cases, the owner requires an operator or, in his absence, the help of a project coordinator to select a location, viability, size of the workable unit, etc., unless the owner belongs to the category (2), (5) from the above.

The owner should take legal advice to ensure that the chosen land is well located and free from legal complications, encumbrances, and zonal problems.

3.2 HELPFUL HINTS FOR THE OWNER

The owner must be fully aware of the challenges in financing, design and planning, construction and finishing, and management of the proposed hotel.

It is necessary to apply proven industrial techniques to ensure that the finished product, of a highly perishable nature sells each day since a hotel is unlike those products, when not sold today, could be sold twice their number the next day, consequently making a profit.

The owner has to be an intelligent businessman who knows how to convert meager resources at his command into a saleable product for his good and also for the good of society. A successful businessman knows how to safeguard their own interest as well as the people who work for them. A Trusteeship approach on behalf of the investors and administrators will go a long way for growth in global terms.

An intelligent businessman has instant solutions to the trouble at hand before it becomes bigger otherwise. In other words, wits and guts are essential requirements. Mr. Radhe Shyam, Chairman of Saraf Group of Industries, used to stress the value of time by citing a colloquial *Marwari* saying, translating roughly to "I am the bride's party. The '*Barat*' is coming". Another saying "Kal kareso aaj, aaj kareso ab", was also oft repeated by him.

In this context, I wish to briefly mention Boris Nikolayevich Lisanevich, a.k.a. Boris Lissanevitch, hotelier and restaurateur of international fame. He was a man ahead of the times who set up the Yak and Yeti restaurant in the Lal Darbar building in Kathmandu in collaboration with Radhe Shyam Saraf. He was a bad businessman commercially.

In business, "how many you know rather than how much you know" also comes into play.

The 'owner's brief' to the design team should be clearly defined so that the outcome is functional and productive when ready, at minimum cost and without compromising on quality. In other words, liberal and complacent attitudes are dangerous at every stage of the project.

3.3 PRELIMINARY WORK

Preliminary work for the owner includes preparing the techno-economic feasibility study, which should be readied by an accountancy consultancy firm specializing in hotel feasibility studies. The feasibility study will bring to light the competition, rates, cost, cash flow, terms and conditions of working in the chosen location, and information about the tourism industry as a whole. The financial and cash flow study should be linked to design, planning, and actual project cost study to safeguard the owner's interest. Such preparation will be by the architect, engineer, and interior designer under the supervision of a project coordinator who will be an independent employee or appointed with the help of the operator if the latter is not already on board. The operator shall give details of every section of the hotel and relate them to costs. The owner should also get the field surveys done as mentioned in Annexure: 02 – Field surveys (Geodesic).

3.4 CHOICE OF THE ARCHITECT

The architect should have the experience of designing at least seven or eight hotels, one or two of which should be in the same area as the owner's location. Unless the architect is well known, it may be advisable to invite competition even if the owner has to compensate those who may not get selected for their work.

The Architect must be committed to the price and not talk in general terms. Some construction companies offer "Design and build" models and if done for a fixed cost, it is worth considering. The owner should never think of becoming a designer himself but rather concentrate on his strengths. The role of the interior designer should be clearly defined. The fee should reflect market standards. Some interior designers tend to become fanciful and expensive, resulting in costly specifications and a consequent increase in cost. Their role, though essential, must be contained within specific parameters. Interior designers should also be given a budget and asked to work within it. They must be told to use local colors and materials as far as possible. The theory of maximum or equivalent must be attained, be it in design or suppliers, to avoid being taken for a ride.

The contractor employed must be proficient in constructing hotels of similar magnitude or even more prominent.

Qualified and experienced engineers should do the mechanical and electrical designs. The contractor involved should be highly technical and professionally oriented. If competent contractors/workers do not execute the mechanical and electrical installations, chances are the clients may walk out, and the hotel itself may go up in flames.

FF&E (Furniture, Fixtures and Equipment) including BOH (Back of the House)/other equipment may come to about 15 to 20% of the project's total cost. Specifications are vital in such cases and should include fire rating, stain repellant rating, etc. It should be noted that the tried and tested designs may also be cheaper and last longer than something new and expensive. The interior designer should be warned about this while designing public areas. The owner should be wary of inferior products being installed by some contractors, especially carpets and curtains.

3.5 HOTEL MANAGEMENT

It is better to go in for well-known management brands like Hyatt, Marriott, Welcome Group, Starwood, etc., even if they seem costlier. In a growing economy, they tend to be more accommodating as there is an opportunity to increase business and, thus, lower overheads. Therefore, it is worth negotiating hard by creating possible competition.

3.6 EQUITY PARTICIPATION

It is to the owner's advantage if the operator can be persuaded to participate in the equity. The operator's head office will watch the performance of the hotel more closely. The percentage of equity may be small yet worthwhile. The management company will get into a technical service agreement with the owner, enabling the owner to use the former's expertise and take advantage of it. The operators have their design standards backed by immense research and development and thus are more modernized. The owner will benefit from the operator's guidance for the software needed in operations. Usually, the management agreements allow the owner a certain degree of freedom to prevent the managing company from expanding their business in the vicinity.

If originality is not tampered with by financial realism, things can go haywire irrespective of the preventive measures. Hence, before signing the management contract, it is better to know the people and their team at the helm to ensure things go well. However, it would be in the owner's interest to have a clause in the contract that in the event of drastic changes in the operators' organization, the owner will be at their liberty to review the agreement.

3.6 INSURANCE

The owner, in his interest, should ensure that the consultants and the project management team have their professional insurance cover to make good any losses the owner may incur because of faults, if any, by the design team or the project manager, in carrying out their responsibilities.

3.7 DISPUTE RESOLUTION

There should be a provision in the contracts between the owner and consultants/project managers regarding dispute resolution in the event of lapses, if any, by any of the parties.

CHAPTER 4

Role of Project Coordinator

4.1 THE ROLE OF PROJECT COORDINATOR

The hotel operator should depute one of his experienced staff members to act as a "Project Coordinator" and charge specific fees. It is also possible that if the owner has not decided on the operator, he would need the services of a "Project Coordinator". In fact, for projects where considerable investment is involved, say a five-star hotel or a resort of 200 or more rooms, the owner must decide on the operator right at the beginning of the project. Owners, in some instances, have had to pay heavily for ignoring this fact. An operator comes into being after years of experience with comprehensive knowledge of the hospitality trade worldwide. They are also well-equipped to create hotels from the concept stage to the completion stage. In reality, an operator is an umbrella as it guarantees the owner a certain percentage of business and ensures thorough management and care of the property. Each operator has their design standards which have to be strictly implemented irrespective of who the owner is.

4.2 QUALIFICATION OF PROJECT COORDINATOR

(*a*) They should have a degree in Hotel Management and/or Tourism Management from a recognized institution.

(*b*) They should have prior experience working in several hotel sites for at least five years.

(*c*) They should have traveled extensively to appreciate the importance of local culture, geographical requirements, atmospheric conditions, and ethnic customs in other parts of the world. These experiences would enable them to visualize a broad picture, the scope of work needed to ensure completion on time, budget, and be functionally modern twenty years hence.

(*d*) They should also have thorough experience in coordinating feasibility studies, including concept and completion of FF&E and BOH (Back of the House viz. kitchen, linear laundry room, stores, staff kitchen, dining & dress changing, lockers, engineering, health club and spa, pantry, wine, cellar, and reception).

1. Role of a Project Coordinator:

(*a*) Assist the owner in arriving at a clear and concise definition of a project and theme to make it a practical reality by blending various disciplines.

(*b*) Deciding with the owner whether the proposed project is:

a business class hotel with maximum simple rooms,

Or

a resort with hotel rooms and suites with multiple cuisines,

Or

a business cum tourist hotel for leisure seeking clients only,

Or

a honeymoon resort,

Or

a spa hotel,

Or

a Golf Resort Hotel.

2. The Project Coordinator is a link between the Owner and:

(*i*) The Architect

(*ii*) The Project Manager

(*iii*) The MEP Consultants

(*iv*) The kitchen & family consultant

(*v*) Food & Beverage Consultant

(*vi*) FF&E Manager

3. Right from the concept stage to the completion of FF&E and commissioning:

(*a*) The project coordinator will assist the owner in analyzing whether the facility could be 24 × 7 or one that closes at a predetermined time.

(*b*) The project coordinator will also assist the owner in deciding project timing, whether to take advantage of local circumstances or consider longer duration in the usual way.

(*c*) The project coordinator will also assist the owner in selecting consultants, including the appointment of a qualified well-known accountancy firm experienced in preparing workable and cost-effective techno-economic feasibility study reports based on the concept given by the architect. The document should be such that it enables the owner to raise funds from financial institutions.

(*d*) The project coordinator will assist the owner's special consultants on the functional design, specifications, and distributions (BOH).

(*e*) The project coordinator is also responsible for the issue of tenders, analysis, orders, and their supervision.

(*f*) FF&E and operating equipment programs and approvals are the project coordinator's responsibility in addition to BOH programs and approvals. The project coordinator should also advise the client on the cost of supplies, FF&E and operational equipment and even the local by-laws.

(*g*) The project coordinator is also responsible for the illumination cost, quality and installation.

(*h*) The project coordinator should be able to decide whether the location:

- Meets the parameters suitable for a hotel
- The number of guest rooms and
- Relevant star category.

(*i*) Complete handover to the Hotel operator.

Summary Checklist Where Project Co-ordinator's Input is Required				
1a	**1b**	**1c**	**2**	**3**
Mock-up	**Guestroom**	**Bathroom**	**BOH**	**FF & E & Operators Equipments**
Carpet/Underlay Installation Accessories Wallpaper/Types Of Adhesive Curtains/ Net Blackout Tracks Method of opening Lighting/ Bedside Table Standard Beds/ Mattress Box Spring Metal Frame Case Goods Bedcover Upholstery/Fabric Scotchguard Fire rating T.V./Remote Ctrl Computer/ Modem TV/ VDUAttachment Pictures Internet Energy Saver	Shape/Size of Type of room Type of Bed Size of Bed Number of Beds Studio Room Furniture Lighting Wardrobe Communication System Computer terminals Telephone with computer Modem+ Printer TV, twospeakers Remote control Functional design of goods Carpet/Underlay Curtains/ Net Blackout Track Wallpaper Pictures	Size of room Size of bath/ USA European Non-slip With/without Jacuzzi Bidet Hairdryer Location Telephone Washing line Shower curtain/Rod One or two basins Basins in Bathroom or Separate area Bath accessories Bottle opener Kleenex box Towel rails/ Shelves	Size of kitchen Type of kitchen Kitchen equipment Size of cold room Size of stores Gas or Electricity Staff restaurant Size of laundry Type of laundry Staff changing room Housekeeping Linen stores Engineering Stores/workshop Saloon Health Club General Stores Strong Room	Computer furniture Fittings and Equipment to be agreed upon To be related to the Class of the hotel The type of user and requirements of the user Operators Equipment Ex: Linen China Glassware Silverware Office Equipment Housekeeping Equipment Guestroom supplies Kitchen Utensils Various categories Of equipment

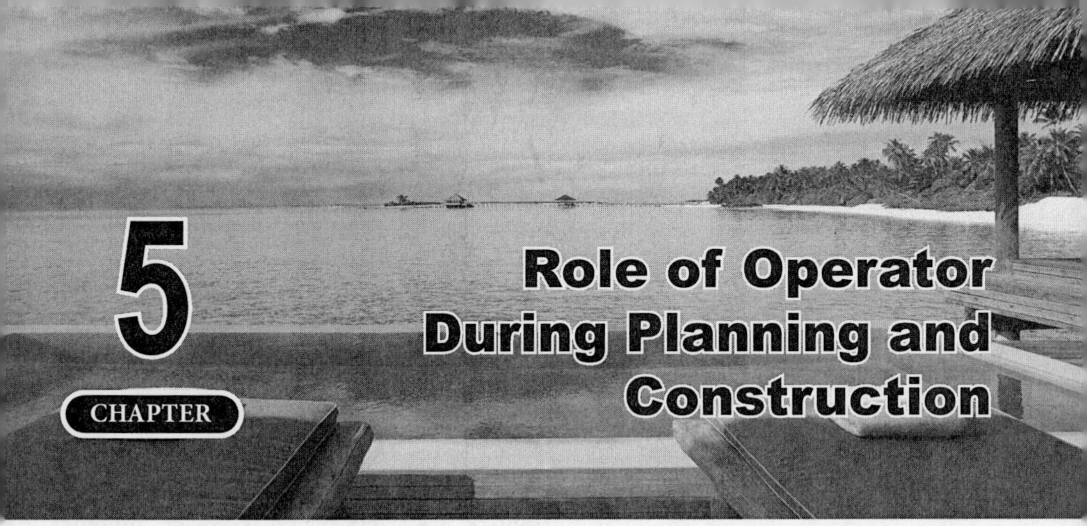

5 CHAPTER
Role of Operator During Planning and Construction

5.1 THE ROLE OF OPERATOR DURING PLANNING & CONSTRUCTION

The operator shall be a leading hotel group like Hyatt, Marriott, etc., who will have their own technical officer in a prominent location where their spread is maximum. It will be usually headed by a person who has considerable experience in operating hotels and setting up new hotels assisted by a planning team comprising professionals in:

1. **Hotel Architecture:** The architect will visit the client units at least once in three months (after initial set up) to review progress and further planning.
2. **MEP Engineering**: Mechanical engineer, experienced in mechanical, electrical and plumbing engineering, will visit the clients for review at least once in three months after initial setup.
3. **FF&E and Food and Beverage:** Available for planning and review.
4. **Business expert:** Available for planning and review.

Based on the Technical Services agreement with the owner, the operator should provide 'Hotel Facilities' list such as:

(*a*) The number of each type of hotel guest rooms.

(*b*) The number and type of food and beverage facilities and banquet and meeting facilities, including the seating capacity of each.

(*c*) The number and type of recreation areas, BOH (Back of the House) areas, administrative areas and retail areas.

(*d*) The operator shall provide the owner a program specification of the recommended size of all hotel facilities in square feet or square meters and shall provide to owner the "Design Guide" based on their standards for use in conceptual plan development.

Follow-up

(*a*) The operator shall go through the conceptual architectural plans of the site plan, floor plan of all typical and non-typical floors, and the development of design, and approve them, including recommendations for improvements, if any.

(*b*) The operator will go through the preliminary architectural plans and specifications consisting of (*a*) Site plan, (*b*) Perspective building sketches or model photographs, (*c*) Floor plans of all floorings indicating the size of each space, (*d*) Building elevations and sections, (*e*) Large scale hotel guest room plans and furnishing layouts, (*f*) Large scale drainage and elevator core and necessary details, (*g*) Vertical transportations analysis, (*h*) Outline specifications for exterior and interior materials and advice on acceptability thereof, with recommendations for improvements, if any.

(*c*) The operator will go through the final plans and specifications consisting of the following:

(*i*) The architectural plans and specifications in sufficient detail for use as "Contract bid and working documents" and submission to appropriate government or regulatory authorities in connection with the application for building permit, zonal variances, fire departmental approvals and other licenses and permits required for construction work.

(*ii*) Drawings for constructing guest room mock-ups.

(*iii*) Lighting and landscaping plans, duly approved by the operator.

(*iv*) Final equipment layouts and specifications, duly approved by the operator.

(*v*) Reproducible rendering of quality and character suitable for making advertising use and approve them with final recommendations for improvement, if any.

5.2 INTERIOR DESIGN AND DECORATION

(*a*) The operator shall select an interior designer subject to the owner's approval.

(*b*) Provide advice and assist in defining the content and manner of presentation of the interior design to be prepared by the designer.

(*c*) Provide advice and technical recommendation to the interior designer on the functional layout of guest rooms, corridors, all public areas and food beverage facilities, ballroom and pre-function spaces.

(*d*) Provide a copy of the "Designer Guide" and "Design Approval Policy" related to interior design to the interior designer.

Follow-up

(*a*) The operator shall go through the preliminary design presentation plans viz. (*i*) Hotel and hotel room layout with indication of location and nature of furniture and furnishings, (*ii*) Perspective room sketches or models or any other means of showing overall design concepts, colors, lighting and materials, (*iii*) Presentation boards samples of floor, wall and ceiling treatment as well as furniture and furnishing materials containing information on flame spread and smoke development and photographs of drawings of furniture, lighting fixtures and accessories, (*iv*) Uniform design and graphics and artwork, and approve the same with recommendations for improvement, if any.

(*b*) Final Design Phase Assistance:

The operator shall go through the final design presentation consisting of: (*i*) Hotel and hotel room layouts including furniture, (*ii*) Elevation and reflected false ceilings plans, lighting, (*iii*) Samples and specifications and fire rating of all floors, walls and ceiling treatments and all furniture and furnishing materials, (*iv*) Details and drawings of specially designed furniture, lighting and fixtures and accessories, photographs of furnishing prototypes, drawings and specifications of hotel guest room mock-ups, uniform graphics and artwork, (*v*) Reproducible renderings of the hotel guest rooms and all public areas of quality and character suitable for marketing and advertising purposes and approve with recommendations for improvement, if any.

(*c*) The operator shall also go through the final detailed working drawings of floor, wall finishes of all types of guest rooms and public areas fit for bid documents/submissions, if any, execution/procurement, etc., including detailed specification of fabrics and approval with recommendations for improvements, if any.

5.3 MECHANICAL AND ELECTRICAL ENGINEERING DESIGN ASSISTANCE

The operator shall make available their design standards concerning any additional or different requirements for (*a*) Heating, ventilation and air conditioning systems, (*b*) Plumbing, drainage disposal or water treatment, (*c*) Electrical power supply and distribution systems in addition to lighting, alarm, radio and telecommunication systems, (*d*) Elevators and escalators, (*e*) Telephone, public address and internal communication systems, (*f*) Building automation systems.

Follow-up

The operator shall go through the preliminary plans and after approval go through the final plans and approve the same with suitable recommendations, if any; and final bid submissions and construction documents concerning them.

1. The operator shall advise the owner on the appointment of a suitable consultant for Life Safety and Fire Protection engineering and provide all guidance in preparing preliminary plans and final execution drawings.
2. Likewise, for
   (*a*) Kitchen, laundry, bar and valet requirement and
   (*b*) Management information integration system:
      (*i*) Advise concerning layout and equipment requirement for (*a*) of above,
      (*ii*) Extent to which technology systems should be used in the hotel based on operational considerations regarding reservations, property management, sales, inventory, guest information, telecommunication, electronic locking & security systems.
3. The operator shall advise on coordination and planning:
   (*a*) Food and Beverage concepts for the hotel
   (*b*) Development of Spa.

Duties of the operator in planning and execution include the role of the project coordinator as described in the earlier chapter and hence not mentioned here. In addition to the installation and commission of plant and equipment, ensuring all maintenance manuals and control system management details are to be made available before taking charge of the finished project.

Chapter 6: Role of Design Team

6.1 INTRODUCTION

This chapter explains the role of the consultants who constitute the design team. The scopes of their activities are:

1. Architecture
2. Structural Engineering
3. Interior Design
4. M.E.P. Equipment
5. Landscaping
6. Illumination
7. Signage & Graphics
8. Kitchen & Laundry
9. Building Automation and
10. Computerization of Hotel Operation

The scope of their activities is described in succeeding chapters.

Role of Architect

6A.1 INTRODUCTION

Architects could be famous firms based in large cities either in India or abroad involved in large projects. In such cases, a local architect is chosen to assist the principal architect in planning, development and detailing. The local architect's role in master planning in such an instance could be between 10% and 50% in design development and documentation. The scope of work of the architect is as follows:

A. Public Areas:

(*a*) Pre-Function Hall
(*b*) Main Banquet Hall (Sub-divisible)
(*c*) Front Office
(*d*) Lobby & Lobby Lounge
(*e*) Circulation & flow Spaces
(*f*) Restrooms - including disability-friendly
(*g*) Elevator Cabins
(*h*) Elevator Lobbies

(*i*) Business Center with Conference Room & IT Stations
(*j*) Coffee shop (24*7) including display Kitchen
(*k*) Specialty Restaurants
(*l*) Fitness Centre
(*m*) Spa
(*n*) Gymnasium
(*o*) Shops.

B. Rooms:

(*a*) Standard/King/Twin/disability-friendly/Guestrooms/Suites (2 types- concept and architectural configuration)
(*b*) Presidential Suite
(*c*) Corridors (Standard and Club Levels)
(*d*) Elevator Lobbies (Standard and Club Levels)
(*e*) Club Lounge with Reception, Coffee Stations, Food Service Stations
(*f*) Lounge & Restrooms
(*g*) Facilities inside the rooms.

C. Back of the House (BOH):

(*a*) House-keeping
(*b*) Laundry
(*c*) Commissary Kitchen and all other Kitchens
(*d*) Staff dining & locker rooms, Toilets
(*e*) Stores
(*f*) Receiving area
(*g*) Plant room
(*h*) Workshop
(*i*) Travel desk.

D. Parking Areas:

(*a*) Basements
(*b*) External
(*c*) Outdoor sports

E. Outdoor facilities:

(*a*) Perimeter wall
(*b*) Swimming pool
(*c*) Jogging track.

Basic Services of Architect Concerning Above Scope of Work

1.0 INITIAL AND FINAL MASTER PLAN

To begin with, the architect will provide the following design services:

1.1 INITIAL MASTER PLAN

Working closely with the client team and its chosen local and international consultants. This will help ensure that the master plan adequately encompasses and acknowledges local history, customs and cultures, and the client's goals and desires.

In this phase, the work involves the development of preliminary layouts for the project, which would include the following tasks:

(*a*) **Background Investigations:** Review all available background information about the project site, including any previous planning studies, climatic patterns, topography and other land characteristics (please see Annexure-02: Field surveys-

Geodesic); regional relationships, access to governmental regulations, existing developmental issues, available infrastructure, past marketing studies, etc. related to the site.

(*b*) **Land Tenure:** Confirm with the client the actual property boundaries and study area of the project.

(*c*) **Development Brief:** Establish a preliminary site development brief or program with the client and his market consultants, indicating appropriate, highest and best uses and activities to be planned on the land consistent with the client's development objectives.

(*d*) **Site Inspection/Analysis:** Conduct in-depth field inspection of the site to identify the environmental setting, principal development constraints and opportunities, overall carrying capacity or optimum level of development, and the most suitable location for the various residential, commercial, open space, recreational and community components.

(*e*) **Preliminary Master Plan:** Prepare three conceptual master plan alternatives for the site, reflecting the principal residential, commercial, community uses, and recreational and access/servicing networks for the overall property.

(*f*) **Selection of Preferred Concept Approach:** Present these preliminary layouts for client review and select a preferred development approach that best meets the client's overall objectives and the anticipated market penetration opportunities. This should also factor in the time and program schedule (trade-wise) for completing the Project (Refer Fig. 3A & 3B–Master Project Schedule – A case study).

1.2 FINAL MASTER PLAN

The intent of the final Master Plan is to refine the preferred master plan concept further. The scope of work would include:

Preliminary Land Use Plan: Following the client's acceptance of a preferred concept approach and its market justification, prepare a Preliminary Land Use Plan for the site. The plan would depict:

(*a*) A land subdivision and circulation plan incorporating the location of the residential, commercial and recreational facilities, plus the principal access, service corridors, vehicular/pedestrian circulation patterns.

(*b*) The areas of support infrastructure and servicing components.

Master Plan: Prepare a Master Plan ("Footprint Plan") for the site, which illustrates the general siting concepts (building footprints) for the principal land uses and structures showing residential uses, recreational elements and other community activities.

Artist's Rendering: Prepare artist's rendering of the overall site to illustrate design character and composition of the site.

Project Description: Prepare a project description that describes each component of the master plan.

Presentation Drawings: Prepare a set of colored presentation drawings depicting the overall development. Work on all plans and drawings is done manually.

Deliverables

The following items will be provided to the client as deliverables:

(*a*) Land Use Plan
(*b*) Master Plan
(*c*) Land Utilization Program
(*d*) Artist's rendering
(*e*) Project Description
(*f*) Booklets of the Master Plan (in A3 size)
(*g*) Overall aerial Perspective
(*h*) Porte cochere Perspective
(*i*) Entire Perspective

2.0 BUILDING CONCEPT, DESIGN DEVELOPMENT & DOCUMENTATION

2.1 CONCEPT

(*a*) **Initial Concept:** The architect will prepare a preliminary concept plan based on an initial site visit and work session with the client. The preliminary concept will be based on the general programmatic brief. It will include an illustrative plan of the main structure, level plans, a preliminary site selection illustrating the relationship of the structures to the topography, a sketch to show the overall architectural character of the project, and an image board.

(*b*) **Final Concept:** The architect will produce a concept package to illustrate the Concept Design. The Concept Plan will include:

1. An illustrative site/roof plan showing all of the components of the project, general landscape recommendations and overall infrastructure elements such as entry driveways and service circulation.
2. Diagrams showing each of the major public levels at 1:500 scale.
3. Site and building cross sections describing vertical relationships at 1:500 scale.
4. Diagrammatic outline elevations of the front and one side of the project to illustrate the project's overall massing and general character.
5. Sketches and vignettes as necessary to describe the architectural character of the project.
6. A written description of the project, including general programmatic information.
7. A gross building area tabulation and schematic plan.

These drawings will be produced manually and colored in a manner suitable for project presentation. Approval of the design direction and area of brief and written authorization to proceed will be given by the owner before the architect commences the project's next phase.

2.2 SCHEMATIC DESIGN

The Architect will:

(*a*) Prepare schematic design drawings based on the approved concept by the client, consisting of drawings and other documents illustrating the scale and relationships of the project in coordination with the services consultants.

(*b*) Prepare a gross building area tabulation based on architect's schematic plan.

(*c*) Will prepare a written description of the schematic design for client's use.

(*d*) Will coordinate its work effort with the client's consultants,who will prepare coordinated design as required and establish the basic design and building systems.

(*e*) The schematic design drawings produced by architect during the schematic design phase will include the following drawings:

	Metric Scale
Site/Roof Plan	1:500
Site Sections	1:500
Floor Plans of All Major Levels	1:200
• Guest Room Blocks	
• Public Areas	
Back of House	1:200
Typical Guest Room & Suite Plans	1:50
Typical Exterior elevations	1:200
Sections	1:200

(*g*) The architect will provide colored perspective sketches to include the following, if required:

— Overall Arial perspective
— Porte cochere perspective
— Entry perspective

(*h*) The architect will also provide the client with one set of reproducible drawings, one copy of the colored perspective sketches, and one copy of the colored site plan.

(*i*) These drawings will be produced digitally using AutoCAD format (latest release) and hand-drawn format at the client's discretion.

2.3 DESIGN DEVELOPMENT

(*a*) Based on the schematic design documents approved by the client and any minor adjustments authorized by the client in the program or project budget, the architect will prepare design development drawings to provide additional detailed information to complete construction documents.

(*b*) Design development drawings will include:

	Metric Scale
Large Scale Sections of Typical Exterior Walls	1:50
Large Scale Partial Exterior Elevations	1:50
Profile Exterior Details	1:50
Finished Schedule for Pubic Areas	
Exterior Materials Board	
Outline Specifications	

(*c*) Architect will provide liaison with local consultants to coordinate balance of design development, if any. Furnish design clarification sketches of major design elements and complete design development package in association with other engineering and specialty consultants.

(*d*) Architect will furnish probable construction cost (*i*) In the concept stage, (*ii*) After initiating bids, (*iii*) After preparing working drawings. These drawings will be produced in a digital format using AutoCAD format (Release 14 or later).

2.4 Construction Documentation

(*a*) Architect will prepare construction documents based on approved design development documents, setting forth in detail the project's architectural construction requirements and time schedule for general construction (As shown in Fig. 2 – General Construction Schedule – A case study). This will include detailed working drawings, floor plans, elevation and sections, partial enlarged detailed plans, interior elevations, finish schedules, hardware schedules, door and window schedules and details, reflected ceiling plan, roof plans, typical wall sections, partition types and details, stair plans, and miscellaneous details.

(*b*) The Architect will provide verification of all local building and plan approval requirements during all phases of the project.

(*c*) Any adjustments to previous preliminary statements of construction cost, indicated by changes in the requirements of general market conditions will be done by the local architect.

2.5 Bid and Tender

The architect will be involved in tender and post-bid negotiation, award of work and periodical supervision and recommend final acceptance and preparation of as-built drawings.

Role of Structural Consultant

6B.1 INTRODUCTION

Responsibilities

1. The consultant shall provide structural design for the project, including design management and coordination, and follow all applicable codes and zonal requirements regarding earthquakes, etc.
2. The consultant shall provide specifications and BOQ for sub-surface investigation.
3. The consultant shall provide specifications, BOQ and tender drawings with soft copies for civil works of structural discipline and working drawings.
4. The consultant shall provide structural analysis for the design, including design data. They shall also provide alternative designs, if necessary, for cost limitations.
5. The consultant will coordinate with the prime consultant (architect) and MEP consultant from time to time.
6. All the stages of work shall be completed by the consultant and shall be as per mutually agreed schedule.

7. The consultant shall advise the client regarding the work under execution during visits to the site and submit periodic reports on his observations.
8. The consultant shall not make any deviation, alteration or omission from the approved drawings, without prior consent from the owner.
9. The consultant shall make the necessary revisions required by the client in the drawings and documents submitted by the consultant at the concept stage.
10. The client shall have the liberty to postpone or not execute any work and the consultant shall not be entitled to any compensation for non-execution of the work except the fees which are payable to the consultant up to the stage of services in progress till then.

Drawing and Documents

The consultant will supply three copies of the Final Report and six sets of relevant drawings (soft copies in AutoCAD Format), including all good-for-construction drawings/prints (architectural) as required by the contractor free of cost.

As-Built Drawings: The consultant will also prepare "As-built" drawings taking into account changes, if any, in carrying out the work.

Role of Interior Designer

6C.1 GOAL

To develop interior planning, design imagery, color schemes, furnishing selections, material and decorative specifications; to review manufacturer's drawings and samples; review plans and recommend planners; and offer consultation in collaboration with other consultants to develop an integrated design, all according to a fixed budget without cost overruns, all in accordance with the phases mentioned below.

Phase-I: Planning:

The interior designer will assist in creating interior layouts and designs that satisfy the client and operator's requirements and recommendations. The interior designer's drawings are to be based on CAD backgrounds submitted by the architect in a mutually acceptable format. The interior designer will establish a basis for developing and implementing the interior design, project schedule, furnishings, fixtures, and artwork budgets. The interior designer will consult with the architect to clearly define the scope of interior design work and design responsibilities.

[Refer "Suggested Provisions for Amenities, Heights, Clearances and Other Valid Suggestions for Star Hotels" in Annexure-06]

Suggested provisions for amenities, heights, clearances and other valid suggestions for services to be provided in star hotels during this phase will include:

- Project-related research
- Program and schedule confirmation
- Room chart and room count analysis
- Square meter/area budget allocations

- Development of schematic floor plans of all areas stipulated in the scope of work will constitute completion of Phase-I (see Chapter-06A: The Role of Architect).

Phase II: Concept

The interior designer will develop their material and furniture selections and interior sketches which will establish the basic design direction. Estimated costs of implementing the interior design concept will be coordinated with the purchasing agent. Services to be provided during this phase will include:

- Development of interior design imagery.
- Presentation of colors and materials.
- FF & E budget review and confirmation.
- Coordination of professional renderings (as required by client).

Phase III: Design Development

Services to be provided will include furnishing sufficient information to the architect and other consultants in AutoCAD format to enable the architect, engineers and other project consultants to incorporate its interior design information into their construction documents and specifications as required. Documents to be submitted to the architect for coordination with other disciplines will include:

- Architectural reference/Floor covering plans
- Furniture/electrical location plans
- Reflected ceiling plans (Showing height, materials and finishes and decorative lighting).
- Concept book to establish design direction for Plumbing/Hardware/Sanitary fittings.

Phase IV: Interior Design Documents

Services to be provided will include the production of the final set of FF&E drawings and specifications,which are intended to provide the basis for purchasing agent's bid documents, product samples, shop drawings, and purchase orders. Documents provided during this phase will include:

- Material Reference/Finish Selection.
- Furnishing Specifications
- Millwork/Joinery Drawings
- Selected Interior Elevations (as required)
- Selected Interior details (as required)
- Miscellaneous Decorative details
- Guest room/Model room documentation for typical king, typical twin and a section of guestroom corridor (one color scheme). Please also see Annexure-04: Guest room items and costing.

Phase V: Prepare Bid Documents, Bid Negotiations, etc.

Services to be provided will include working with the purchasing agent, contractors and manufacturers in reviewing bids, assisting in the negotiations, and making reasonable adjustments to meet previously established budgets. Services to be provided during this phase will include:

- Assistance in pre-qualification of vendors.
- Assistance in the evaluation of pricing
- Documentation of Budget required design revisions

Phase VI: Design Implementation

This phase will include periodic visits to the project site to review if work is being performed in accordance with interior designer's documents, specifications and design concepts. Services to be provided during this phase will also include:

- Review of purchase orders.
- Review of shop drawings.
- Review of samples and/or prototypes.
- Installation review.

Role of ME&P Engineers

1.0 SCOPE OF SERVICES

Services in connection with the project are engineering and technical consultancy services related to the planning and designing of engineering services mentioned as below:

1.1 ELECTRICAL, IT AND NETWORK ENGINEERING

(*a*) Electrical distribution network for landscape lighting, external illumination, power outlet, fountain, car calling system, etc.

(*b*) Public Address System

(*c*) Power requirements including HT, LT, DG, etc., supported by necessary calculations.

(*d*) General lighting and power layout for all areas considering illumination levels as per BIS code and as per owner's requirements. The layout shall include conduit layout, wiring details, switching details, etc.

(*e*) Layout for CCTV, telephone, cable networking, etc.

(*f*) Earthing and lightning protection layout.

(*g*) External and internal lighting and power engineering.

(*h*) Specifications for all conduits, network elements, switches, cables, fixtures, fittings and installations, etc., as mentioned in the design.

(*i*) Infrastructure of complete electrical and networking services, including routings, locations, etc., showing hook-up points in the entire area.

1.2 Plumbing and Sanitary Services

(*a*) Water requirements, water usage pattern, disposal of excess water, water conservation schemes, etc., supported by necessary calculations for different areas.

(*b*) Design of water distribution, storage and recycling system.

(*c*) Design of cold/hot water piping, internal waste and sewage piping, and rainwater piping.
(*d*) Design and layout of external stormwater disposal system.
(*e*) Design and layout of sewerage systems.
(*f*) Specification of plumbing and sanitary fittings and fixtures.
(*g*) If applicable, pool filtration and water treatment plant, including water bodies.
(*h*) Hot water storage and recycling of the same in totality.
(*i*) STP (Sewage Treatment Plant) location.

1.3 External Services

(*a*) Sewer lines up to treatment plant/town sewer.
(*b*) Water supply external distribution and tube wells, etc.
(*c*) Stormwater disposal.
(*d*) Water supply to garden hydrant systems (Garden hydrant systems shall be designed by the landscape architect).

1.4 HVAC System

(*a*) Heat load calculations and cooling load estimates based on air conditioning system to be adopted.
(*b*) Ventilation scheme for toilets, kitchens and basements with temperature conditions, necessary air changes as per statutory requirements, etc.
(*c*) Specifications for all fixtures, fittings, and installations of piping, pumps, chillers, etc., forming a part of the HVAC system in the project.
(*d*) Air Conditioning.
(*e*) Heating.
(*f*) Mechanical Ventilation.
(*g*) Power and cooling water supply to Refrigeration Systems for Cold Storage/Deep Freezers (Cold Storage and Deep Freezers shall be designed and specified by the Kitchen consultant).
(*h*) Clean room applications like computer rooms and electronics.

A comparison for various types of systems needs to be submitted along with cost comparison, efficiency of the system, energy consumption per unit of cooling, advantages and disadvantages.

1.5 Security Systems & Fire Fighting Services

(*a*) Design of fire protection system as per the requirements of FM, UL Codes/Indian Standard Codes/NBC
(*b*) Design and layout of fire alarm systems.
(*c*) Integration/design of security systems as per guidelines provided by the owner, along with necessary integrated services' construction documents.
(*d*) Specifications for all items and installations of all equipment including electrical requirement for control, forming a part of the fire safety, fire alarm system and fire fighting services.

(*e*) Automated parking control system.

(*f*) Access control and CCTV system.

1.6 Gas Bank & Fuel Storage

(*a*) Design for storage and usage/dispensing methods for various areas of the commercial area, complying with rules and regulations for storage and usage. All the design and related parameters to be provided by the facility planner (any services in terms of the drainage, electric, piping, as per requirements) shall be designed by the operator.

(*b*) Oil tank, pumps and piping.

1.7 Building Management Systems

Design of building management systems for integration of utilities for efficiency of operations and optimizing energy use, input and output summary, the architecture of building management systems, working strategy, BOQ specification, and conservation of resources.

1.8 Kitchen & Laundry System

(*a*) Design of kitchen and laundry (services only)

(*b*) Specification of equipment (ventilation, electrical, water supply & disposal)

(*c*) Identification and recommendation of vendors

(*d*) Budgeting and costing

1.9 Boiler House

(*a*) Design of the boiler house.

(*b*) Hot water boiler P&I (Protection & Indemnity).

(*c*) Schematic layout of boiler room with piping.

(*d*) Heat recovery & serve system from heat pump.

(*e*) Specification of equipment.

(*f*) Identification and recommendation of vendors.

(*g*) Budgeting and costing.

1.10 Data and Telecom Services

(*a*) Design of data and telecommunication system (Circuit elements switches, panels, hubs, UPS, etc.)

(*b*) Schematic layout for data and telecommunication systems.

(*c*) Specifications of equipment requirement.

(*d*) Identification and recommendation of vendors.

(*e*) Budgeting and costing.

1.11 Water Treatment System

(*a*) Design of water treatment system.

(*b*) Schematic layout of water treatment plant room with piping.

(*c*) P&I Diagram.

(*d*) Specification of equipment, piping & dosing.

(*e*) Identification and recommendation of vendors.

(*f*) Budgeting and costing.

1.12 Waste Handling & Disposal System

All the design and related parameters are to be provided by the facility planner. (Any services in terms of the drainage, electric, piping as per requirements) shall be designed by the operator.

(*a*) Design of system

(*b*) Approval for disposal/incineration system

(*c*) Flow process diagram

(*d*) Identification, segregation and disposal of waste.

1.13 Music/TV Systems

(*a*) Layout and distribution

(*b*) Satellite dish antennae receiving equipment

(*c*) Other equipment associated with the system, piped music system

1.14 Sound Systems

Power supply to sound reinforcement systems for banquet halls and public address system for guest rooms.

1.15 Lift System

(*a*) Lift system for guests and staff, service and freight.

(*b*) Specifications of equipment.

(*c*) Identification and recommendation of vendors.

1.16 Mechanical Services

(*a*) Basement drainage pumping system.

(*b*) Water supply pumping systems, fire fighting pumping systems.

(*c*) Water treatment plant.

1.17 Disaster Management System

All the design and related parameters to be provided by signage consultant/facility planner in consultation with architect (any services in terms of the electric points, etc.).

(*a*) Preparation of disaster management system considering occupational usage levels of various buildings forming the commercial area.

(*b*) Plan should show the evacuation route, the time for evacuation, and the safe assembly area for the occupants in the event of any disaster.

(*c*) Consultant to implement an evacuation drill methodology and coordinate with the concept consultant to incorporate the plan in the design of the various buildings under commercial area.

1.18 Contract Services

To prepare design, finalize with owner and provide the general conditions and special conditions of contract. To provide final technical specifications, cost estimates, budgets, detailed bill of quantities and tender documents for engineering and design services along with analysis and justification. This service shall also include analysis and evaluation of contractors for shortlisting, pre-qualification of contractors/sub-contractors/suppliers etc., pre-bid meetings with contractors, issue of notice inviting tenders (NIT), tender documents, tender opening with owner, participate in negotiation meetings, preparation of techno-commercial comparative analysis statement for the bids at various stages of the tender award process, recommendation and assistance to owner for the award of contract.

1.19 Construction/Sanction Documents Services

(*a*) To prepare as per the prevailing local bye-laws and in coordination with the principal architect/professionals appointed by the owner, the general construction M.E.P.(Engineering Services), F.F.&E. and all other works and other documents of adequate number of sets required for approval from relevant authorities and make necessary alterations and corrections in the submission plans and documents, if required by the sanctioning authority during the sanctioning process.

(*b*) To prepare drawings and documents of adequate number of sets that the authorities may require for approval during the progress and completion of the project.

(*c*) To prepare and provide the final working drawings for works of adequate number of sets that will detail the requirements for the entire project's construction. This shall include preparation of sketches/drawings for any alteration, revision or variation during construction and provide revised drawings incorporating such changes.

(*d*) To coordinate with the specially appointed consultant and give recommendations on materials, samples, mock-ups, fabrication/shop drawings and design calculations provided by the contractor.

(*e*) To check and give recommendations on extra/additional/alternate items submitted by the contractor for the engineering services works.

(*f*) To inspect the works during periodic site visits/inspections and issue necessary instructions for rectification of works not conforming to the engineering and design requirements.

(*g*) On completion of the building block/phase/project, inspect the works; assist in preparing a benchmark defects list for rectification by the contractor and issue completion certificate on satisfactory completion after removal/rectification of defects.

(*h*) On completion of the building block/phase/project, prepare the completion plans and other documents for obtaining the occupation/completion certificate from the relevant sanctioning authority.

(*i*) On completion of the project, the consultant shall provide two sets of Compact Disks (CDs)/pendrive containing all latest/final construction and completion drawings drawn on the AutoCAD program.

1.20 Coordination Services

(*a*) Consultant shall depute a team of engineers to coordinate with the local authorities, architects/engineers at the time of making corrections in submission drawings and documents in accordance with requirements of the sanctioning body.

(*b*) To coordinate all basic services as mentioned above and integrate the same with those of local authority, including active coordination with government bodies/authorities through the liaison architect/professionals appointed by the owner, various specialized consultants, contractors and owner, etc., on the best delivery approach for the project. To design, prepare and provide the coordinated plans and drawings for overlapping/conflicting services, clearly showing the levels, details of their placement and interrelationship with civil structure, finishing and other services.

(*c*) To ensure high quality and documents, the consultant shall regularly interact with the project manager through periodic meetings.

(*d*) To coordinate and provide all possible assistance to the owner and the appointed liaison architect/professionals in dealing with relevant Govt. bodies/authorities.

(*e*) Integration of the existing hotel engineering services with the new project.

1.21 Statutory Approvals Services

(*a*) The consultant shall prepare and submit drawings, documents and certificates necessary for submission to statutory bodies for sanction and assist and advice on formalities, including giving necessary inputs/incorporating necessary changes for approval by statutory bodies, until the final approvals (including the completion/occupation certificate) are obtained. The consultant shall coordinate with the owner-appointed specialized consultant to prepare detailed design of plumbing, drainage, electrical, HVAC and other engineering service systems as required by the authorities.(Please see Annexure: 08 for List of Statutory & Local Body approvals required)

(*b*) The deliverables by the consultant for this service shall include the following:

  (*i*) Integration of drawings of external services for plumbing and drainage for the entire complex/project.

  (*ii*) Design coordination and integration of detailed drawings and complete scheme for local authorities/fire authorities showing all fire services.

  (*iii*) Design coordination and integration of detailed drawings and complete scheme for local authorities/electricity department showing all electrical services.

  (*iv*) Detailed drawings and complete scheme for Aviation department and any other statutory body showing required details.

  (*v*) Design coordination and integration of services for internal development plan as required by the authorities.

(*vi*) Coordination for detailed design report and calculations of the services mentioned above, as required by authorities.

(*vii*) Provide assistance to the owner and the appointed liaison architect/ professionals in obtaining all the approvals from the relevant authorities.

(*viii*) The consultant shall provide various basic services mentioned above during different stages of work. A few of these stages may repeat or overlap depending upon the approval process, marketing requirements, construction phasing, and overall construction schedule.

The consultant shall coordinate with other owner-appointed consultants and agencies approved by the owner (herein referred to as sub-consultants) and establish with these other agencies the detailed scope of services and necessary schedules for inputs required for the timely completion of the subject package.

The consultant shall be responsible for the integrated design, layouts and details for all services like roads, MEP services and other infrastructure within the plot boundary of the commercial area, based on the design criteria provided by the owner.

The consultant, in consultation with hotel operator's technical services, shall develop and agree to a schedule with specific milestones/timelines for completion of construction of the building including targeted dates for delivery of plans and specifications to hotel operators technical services as contemplated under this agreement and approval periods for review of such plans and specifications by hotel operator's technical services.

2.0 SCHEDULE OF SERVICE

2.1 Preliminary Stage

The consultant shall consult with the project manager, owner, prime consultant/architect, interior designer, and any additional pertinent consultants to ascertain the project's specific requirements.

(*a*) Render advice to the project manager, owner, prime consultant/architect on the engineering services to be provided, space allocation for cable risers, pipe, ducts, equipment, etc. as are required for the systems enumerated above and setting of standards and specifications of works to be adopted in line with the guidelines of international standards for operational requirements.

(*b*) Render advice to the project manager, owner/prime consultant on plant room requirements and structural requirements for all elements of the system.

(*c*) Assist the project manager, owner/architect by preparing preliminary drawings and by holding discussions with appropriate authorities, wherever necessary, to obtain statutory approvals as necessary and required.

(*d*) Submit a detailed report to the project manager, owner/prime consultant/architect on services describing concept with proper technical and cost-benefits analysis, recommendations and cost estimates.

(*e*) Submit a system design including cost estimate and a time schedule for the completion and submission of drawings and necessary design documentation for approval by the project manager. The designs are subject to a prior review if so desired by the owner.

2.2 Schematic Design Stage

(*a*) Carry out comprehensive HVAC, electrical load calculations and computation for total water requirement.

(*b*) Preparation of preliminary drawings, identifying the external services, size and location of plant rooms, AHU rooms, ventilation fan rooms; substation; low voltage system control room; water tanks, pump room, fire fighting pump room, water treatment plant, and sewage treatment plant (unless the existing plant capacity permits) including holding discussions with appropriate authorities whenever necessary for obtaining required statutory approvals as required.

2.3 Design Development Stage

The consultant shall:

(1) Prepare detailed design and tender drawings, including layout drawings incorporating all elements of the services as given in the scope of work 1.0. The consultant agrees that the designs are subject to prior review by the owner at his discretion.

(*b*) Coordinate the details and drawings with the project manager, owner/architect at his discretion.

(*c*) All drawings and specifications shall be submitted to the project manager in accordance with the agreed time schedule. The design schedule shall allow sufficient time for the project manager to review all drawings and specifications.

(*d*) The design schedule shall be updated every fortnight to reflect the actual progress on the project and revisions to the project master schedule. Revisions to the design schedule shall be subject to the project manager's prior written approval.

(*e*) The consultant shall cooperate fully with the project manager in analyzing value-engineering proposals, which relate to or affect the design. Any such value engineering proposals accepted by the project manager shall be fully coordinated and integrated into the drawings and specifications by the consultant.

2.4 Tendering and Bidding Stage

(*a*) This stage shall commence with the approval of design development drawings, documents and estimates by the owner. The consultant shall prepare the bidding documents for all the buildings and services stated above and coordinate engineering services with other owner-appointed consultants based on the approved designs.

(*b*) During this stage, the consultant shall jointly with the architect/project manager, establish the extent and scope of the contract documents.

(*c*) The consultant shall also coordinate all specialized consultants' documents and incorporate them into the contract document packages.

(*d*) The consultant shall conduct preliminary pre-qualification analysis of the prospective contractors, sub-contractors, and suppliers in association with the owner and shortlist competitive agencies.

(*e*) A draft set of contract documents shall be sent to the project manager and the owner for their comments and clarifications regarding technical, commercial, legal and design issues. These clarifications and comments shall be suitably incorporated in the final draft contract documents, which shall get approved by the owner.

(*f*) After approval from the project manager and the owner, the consultant shall commence the tendering and bidding process. The work associated with this shall include coordinating the pre-bid meetings with the pre-qualified contractors and clarifying their queries over technical, commercial issues and tender drawings.

(*g*) On receipt of the bids, the consultant shall open the same jointly with the owner. The consultant shall evaluate the bids received and obtain clarifications from the bidders on points of confusion or incorrect information. They shall thoroughly review all bids received, for missing information, exclusions and deviations.

(*h*) The consultant shall prepare the tender analysis and techno-commercial comparative statements for the bids received. Comparative statements will include quantifiable cost implications for the conditions specified by the contractor.

(*i*) The consultant shall prepare agenda for negotiations with each contractor and assist and provide all necessary inputs to the project manager and the owner, as required, to negotiate with the contractors on cost and contract conditions. They shall prepare the minutes of the meeting and seek confirmation on minutes of negotiation meetings from each contractor to quantify the same in terms of cost implication, if any.

(*j*) On the basis of final confirmation from the contractors, the consultant shall prepare the final techno-commercial comparative statement and forward them to the project manager and the owner along with this report and recommendations for the award of the contract.

(*k*) The consultant shall assist the project manager and the owner in selecting the contractors for award of contract.

(*l*) The deliverables by the consultants for this stage shall include the following:

(*i*) Notice inviting tender.

(*ii*) Instructions to bidders.

(*iii*) Detailed scope of work.

(*iv*) Bills of quantities along with the control estimates, quantities, rates and amounts.

(*v*) Assistance in analysis of market-rate items.

(*vi*) Detailed general and technical specifications of the works.

(*vii*) For specialized jobs required as per the manufacturer's specifications, product data and manufacturer's specifications.

(*viii*) List of approved makes and brands.

(*ix*) General conditions of the contract.

(*x*) Special conditions of the contract.

(*xi*) Bidding/tender drawings detailed to the required parameters.

(*xii*) Approved proforma/formats for agreement, performance bond, deviation from technical specifications, and conditions of the contract, bank guarantees, indenture for secured advance, extra item and change order form, quality and safety assurance plans.

(*xiii*) Approved samples of the materials/fittings/fixtures property fitted on display boards through contractor/vendors.

(*xiv*) Six sets of final contract agreement documents executed with the selected contractor(s) properly bound in a book form.

The tendering and bidding stage shall be deemed complete (work/building/phase-wise) on the award of all the contracts for that building/phase.

2.5 Execution Stage/Construction Stage and Commissioning Stage

(*a*) The consultant shall submit a comprehensive list of drawings to be issued for the project, along with the issuance schedule. Supervise the construction and commissioning, and prepare "As-Built" drawings upon completion of the work.

3.0 SCOPE OF CIVIL DESIGN ENGINEERING/ARCHITECTURE

3.1 Services During Concept Phase

(*a*) Onsite utility system

(*b*) Off-site utility system

(*c*) Fire prevention system

(*d*) Drainage (Stormwater)

(*e*) Paving, compound walls, roads, waterbodies and retaining walls

3.2 Services during Design Development Phase

Binding in the work done in the seventh phase, the contractor will establish the final scope and preliminary details for on-site and off-site end works. Outline specifications and materials used will also be prepared.

The construction phase consists of final engineering calculation drawings and specifications based on the approved design development document. This sets into detail civil construction requirements for the hotel. Design for access roads, water bodies, compound walls, retaining walls, parking areas and drawings will be carried out on the computer system (CAD), including built drawings.

Role of Landscape Design Architect: Illumination

1.0 ROLE OF LANDSCAPE DESIGN ARCHITECT

(*a*) Coordination with other architects and consultants.

(*b*) Preliminary studies, including soil survey, water resources, etc.

Concept Phase: Material consideration of alternative systems and equipment and development of conceptual design solutions for landforms, lawns, plantings pro-green requirements, physical site characteristics, design objective and environmental requirements.

This will be carried out in close conjunction with the architectural design. If required, a three-dimensional model will be prepared.

Design development phase will include the development of client-approved concepts to a finished product, including outline specifications to be included in bid documents. The work will also include assistance in the preparation of bid documents, bid negotiations, construction supervision and review of finished work.

Final Phase: The work will include the final preparations of drawings and specifications based on the design development documents. This sets out in detail the landscape requirements of the project.

Outcome: All lawns, pathways, water bodies, cascades, lift irrigation systems, fountains, under water lightings, pathway lighting, swimming pool surroundings, steps and ramps outdoor sports, boundary fence, interior planters, etc.

Construction phase: Preparation of basic bid documents, including drawings and specifications, past tender negotiations, construction supervision coordination with other consultants included.

2.0 ROLE OF ILLUMINATION CONSULTANT

Illumination consultant should have vast experience in hotels and resorts illumination, international norms, latest advancements in illuminations systems such as the use of LED lights, dimmers, etc.

The illumination expert comes in when all the interior and exterior structural and architectural details are in place.

Areas covered:

(*a*) Guest Room lighting
(*b*) Suite lighting
(*c*) Lobby lighting.
(*d*) Bar lighting
(*e*) Lift lobby lighting
(*f*) Restaurant lighting
(*g*) Banquet hall lighting
(*h*) Ball room lighting
(*i*) Lighting of external lawns, building exterior
(*j*) Rendezvous space
(*k*) Common areas
(*l*) Parking areas (surface)
(*m*) Pool and water bodies lighting
(*n*) Outdoor sports areas
(*o*) Façade & external lighting

Exterior lighting mostly concealed should be able to define the architecture of the buildings, including neon signs.

3.0 SIGNAGE AND GRAPHICS CONSULTANT

When a customer checks into the hotel room,s/he can see signage on the back of the door that tells the exact location of the room vis a vis the fire escape. As one sees on the room desk, a guide book informs the customer of the facilities available in the hotel and the room service menu. Information includes the food outlets (restaurants), the spa, the fitness centre and audio-visual facilities. The restaurants have menu cards giving details of food available and the timings. The front office also provides enough literature to acquaint one with the programme in the banquet hall and details of the meeting rooms. All these are prepared by the signage & graphics specialist.

Role of Kitchen and Laundry Consultants

1.1 ROLE OF KITCHEN AND LAUNDRY CONSULTANT

The kitchen and laundry consultant will advise the owner in setting up various types of kitchens involved in the hotel depending on the number of rooms, banquet facilities, specialty restaurants, etc. They will coordinate with the operator, principal architect and service consultants as to the size and location of the kitchens and the laundry. Invariably the kitchens are adjoining the restaurants, except the commissary kitchen, which is located centrally to be of service to the other kitchens. In addition to the restaurant kitchens, room service kitchen will be attached to a multi-cuisine restaurant, 24 × 7 Coffee shop kitchen. The commissary kitchen where all raw materials are processed will consist of the butchery, the deep freezer, walk-in cold rooms, stores, bakery, vegetable processing section, etc. This work includes display kitchens also.

The kitchen and laundry consultant will also decide on the equipment needed considering the size of the hotel and the number of washing machines, the ironers and the extent of power, water, gas services required. They will also prepare all the detailed drawings. The operator, food and beverage expert, will be closely involved in the setting up and commissioning of the kitchen equipment.

The kitchen and laundry consultant will also assist the owner in preparing bids, bid negotiations, quality and cost control and final installation and commissioning of the equipment.

Building Automation Systems & Digitization of Hotel Operations

1.1 INTRODUCTION

A. **Building Automation System**: Three levels of controls:
   (*a*) Operation control
   (*b*) Supervisory control
   (*c*) Direct digital control

B. **Standby Energy Management Strategy**:

(*a*) Chiller sequencing

(*b*) Chill water temperature reset

(*c*) Lead/Lag control

(*d*) Demand limiting

(*e*) Land rolling

(*f*) Optimal start/stop

(*g*) Customer specific programme, etc.

C. **Areas of HVAC**:

(*a*) Central chiller water system

(*b*) Ventilation and exhaust system

(*c*) Treated fresh air AHUs

(*d*) Public area AHUs

(*e*) Electrical D.G. set

(*f*) HVAC monitor control

(*g*) Electrical system

(*h*) Lifts

(*i*) Plumbing installation

D. **Computerisation of Hotel Operations**: Many hotels that have computerized their operations have done so only for their front office operations and not proceeded further. Reasons vary from unavailability of technology, device drivers and hardware interface to divergent technologies while starting their establishments. Advancements in client-server computing, availability of universal software for total computerization integrating wireless networking, fire alarm systems, building automation systems, ability to design and implement device drivers allow them to receive and share information from client systems across various locations of the hotel.

Automation requires the system to contact and communicate with the hotel's staff wherever they may be and give them assignments (i.e.,duties). Automation also requires the system to monitor staff performance and report to higher authorities when an assigned task is not completed within the set time. Only then would one be able to establish and maintain service standards.

The central server should have the ability to capture data as work happens in real-time. Their process control interface, i.e., automation software to measure temperature, time, etc., should be reliable, periodic and accurate than manual systems. There should not be a need to enter data through the keyboard alone.

Current automation packages for hotels provide communicative and interactive capabilities that help run the different back of the house operations and other departments efficiently, starting from the engineering and house-keeping departments. The tasks being done by every staff member are monitored and reported to the managers online. The selected system should monitor the operations till each task is complete. Managers may be out of the hotel and still access their profile using "Remote Access" (modules) from any computer terminal. For those on the move, a wireless network connection to laptops or the use of smartphones is advisable.

Some of the important modules of client-server software are:

- Front office operations
  - (*a*) Reservations
  - (*b*) Cancellations (and re-booking)
  - (*c*) Check-in
  - (*d*) Room Assignment (Room re-assignment)
  - (*e*) Wake-up calls
  - (*f*) Check-outs
  - (*g*) Time office (for staff attendance and presence monitoring)
- Financial accounting
  - (*a*) Client accounting/Billing
  - (*b*) Telephone interface
  - (*c*) Room service, restaurant and bar orders
  - (*d*) Messages
  - (*e*) E-mails
  - (*f*) Task Manager

Any other modules

Back of the House Operations

(*a*) Corrective maintenance system

(*b*) Schedule maintenance system

(*c*) Fire alarm interface

(*d*) Building automation

(*e*) Interfaces to pagers

(*f*) Interfaces to EPABX system

(*g*) Interfaces to CTI system

(*h*) E-mail (Local and internet)

(*i*) Interactive TV

(*j*) Interface to lift systems

(*k*) Interface to ECR and POS systems.

(*l*) Interface to electronic locks (CISA, SAVELOCK VINGCARD, etc.)

(*m*) Room management system

(*n*) Butler paging

(*o*) Room refresh services

(*p*) Banquet management system

(*q*) Chief operations.

(*r*) Staff appearance monitor.

Some of the best operating systems are:

(*a*) Electra cloud-based hotel management system

(*b*) PMS software

(*c*) Fidelis hotel management system.

Building Information Model (BIM)

This software creates a virtual 3D model of the design of the building along with all the service infrastructure. This makes the work of the architect, engineer and various professionals collaborative, automated and productive.

Building information model (BIM) is an intelligent 3D-model-based process that gives architecture, engineering, and construction professionals the insight and tool to go through the project cycle more efficiently, i.e., plan, design, construct and manage building and infrastructure.

The aim is to digitize complete project data from concept to finish. It increases the quality, transparency, cost, and schedule security of construction projects.

This describes a method of optimized planning, execution and administration of building objects with the help of appropriate software. All the relevant building data is recorded digitally, and the building is visualized as a "Digital Twin."

BIM brings all those involved in the project together on one platform starting from the planning phase,thus saving many coordination steps. BIM uses intelligence by connected work flows to help improve predictability, productivity and profitability. BIM improves MEP (Mechanical, electrical & plumbing) design quality and helps collaborate in real-time to support the on-time progress and completion of the project.

Due to the common database used by BIM, every change or correction is implemented automatically in the entire construction plan. It is transparent and comprehensive for all the related professionals involved in the project.

BIM also enables professionals to simulate and test the design/drawings in the virtual model so that errors and inconsistency can be detected early and eliminated easily. BIM can be used not only in the construction industry but also in ongoing operations and facility management.

To Sum Up, BIM helps

- To enhance planning, design and delivery of scalable and sustainable civil infrastructure with a full range of tools.
- Visually expose project constructability, manage project cost-effectively and better project outcomes.
- A very efficient and effective means for smooth coordination amongst all the stakeholders from beginning to end of the project due to a single common digital platform.

CHAPTER 7 Project Management/ Construction Management

1.0 PRELIMINARIES

After the decision of the owner to appoint a project manager in consultation with the operator, necessary arrangements must be made to house the project manager and his staff with all the required tools. After estimating the team required, they should be recruited and assigned respective duties. As the volume and nature of the project are clear from the feasibility report, the consultants, including the architect (principal consultant), should be brought on board and thereafter, project management should follow the cardinal principles laid down by established procedures, including trial and error methods.

The definition, history, techniques of project management such as PERT and CPM are mentioned in detail in Chapter-01 (Introduction).

1.1 PREVIEW OF SCOPE OF SERVICES OF PROJECT MANAGEMENT

The project manager should be a passionate and responsible individual focused on professional management of high order with sufficient experience of similar projects. With a successful track record, he should deliver the project on time, within budget and to the highest level of quality.

1.2 GOALS

The agency should have three primary goals for the project construction management services:

(*a*) To ensure that design intent and construction quality standards are achieved.
(*b*) To ensure that the project schedule is met.
(*c*) To ensure that the project is completed within the budget.

To achieve these goals, the managers and staff of the Agency selected should focus on the following with suitable software (Primavera or Microsoft):

(*a*) Prepare a schedule for general construction - M.E.P. and F.F.&E.
(*b*) Establish design management and document control for procedures.
(*c*) Establish quality control procedures.
(*d*) Establish cost control procedures.
(*e*) Establish program control procedures.
(*f*) Establish reporting and communication procedures.

1.3 TASKS

The Agency thus selected should ensure the following:

(*a*) With suitable software Primavera or Microsoft, prepare a schedule of general construction and one for the whole project including M.E.P., F.F.& E., landscaping, signage & graphics and building automation.

(*b*) Establish design management and document control procedures.

(*c*) Establish cost control procedures.

(*d*) Establish time and programme control procedures.

1.4 MASTER PLAN

The project manager will ensure that architect will spend at least two weeks at the site and will work closely with the client's team and its chosen local and international consultants. This ensures that the master plan adequately encompasses and acknowledges the local history, customs and cultures of the place and the client's goals and desires. The preliminary project layout will be developed, which includes:

(*a*) Background investigation

(*b*) Land tenure

(*c*) Development brief

(*d*) Site inspection analysis and

(*e*) Selection of preferred project approach.

1.5 KICK-OFF MEETING

As and when the architect prepares three conceptual master plans, alternatives reflecting principal residential, commercial and community use, in addition to recreational access, servicing to the property with approximate estimates, a kick-off meeting is held, preferably at the operator's technical head quarters, to review the three alternatives and select the most suitable one and take the following decisions vis-à-vis the project, i.e., the project goals namely:

(*a*) Functional content of the project

(*b*) Budget estimate

(*c*) Type of interior architecture preferred.

(*d*) Project schedule

(*e*) Consultant – Owner - Operator liaison.

(*f*) Potential contract options (e.g., Turnkey)

(*g*) The operator's design standard to be followed by the consultants (design team).

(*h*) Electrical, mechanical service requirements.

(*i*) Potential sources for the equipment suppliers.

(*j*) Set the dates for key project outputs, such as schematic cost estimates.

2.0 THE CLIENT BRIEF

The Project management team will have several meetings with the owner to understand the owner's point of view or what usually is called "owner's brief." - an outline of the project, taking into account building function, space requirement and usage, site information, cost targets, time and quality targets, occupational requirements, and commercial objectives.

The project manager will monitor the development of the outline brief into a detailed brief with the proposed design team.

The project manager will select the design team by mutual consultation with the owner and the principal architect, the operator (if already on board), taking into account their suitability, experience, etc.

3.0 OWNER'S BRIEF REVIEW

After reviewing the detailed "owner's brief" with the design team, the project manager will advise the client of contractual feasibility and procurement within the cost and time parameters.

4.0 OVERALL STRATEGY OR MASTER PROGRAMME

The project manager will prepare a master program setting out the management approach for the project with the basic project structure, the role of project participants, and mechanisms to plan, execute, monitor, and review the project development according to the client brief and overall Project duration and key milestones.

5.0 PHASING STUDIES

The project manager will analyze the impact of financing on (*a*) Design, (*b*) Procurement, (*c*) Construction and (*d*) Commissioning requirements of various phasing options.

6.0 CONTRACTUAL COST ESTIMATES

The project manager will prepare the contractual cost estimates based on the conceptual design of the design team based on the elemental cost estimates or the basics of the project model. The architect and other consultants will prepare the cost estimates for each stage for their scope of work.

7.0 PROCUREMENT STRATEGY

Considering specific project conditions vis-à-vis time, design, local and international variables, long lead-time deliverables, local requirements, site-wide purchasing opportunities and standard contract documentation, the project manager should develop a strategy to procure work either on a turn-key basis or split trade-wise, i.e., general construction and services separately.

The project manager will also consult with the owner whether to commence construction after completing the design documentation or progressively.

8.0 PROJECT MANAGEMENT ORGANISATION STRUCTURE AND STAFF DUTIES

8.1 Project organization structure, responsibilities and reporting relations are enclosed in Fig. 1: Organigram– Project Management. The overall staff required depends on the project's scope (as desired above) and the complexities involved. The adage "horses for courses" has a broad connotation and meaning. The staff requirement, i.e., the numbers depend on the stage of the work and discipline involved.

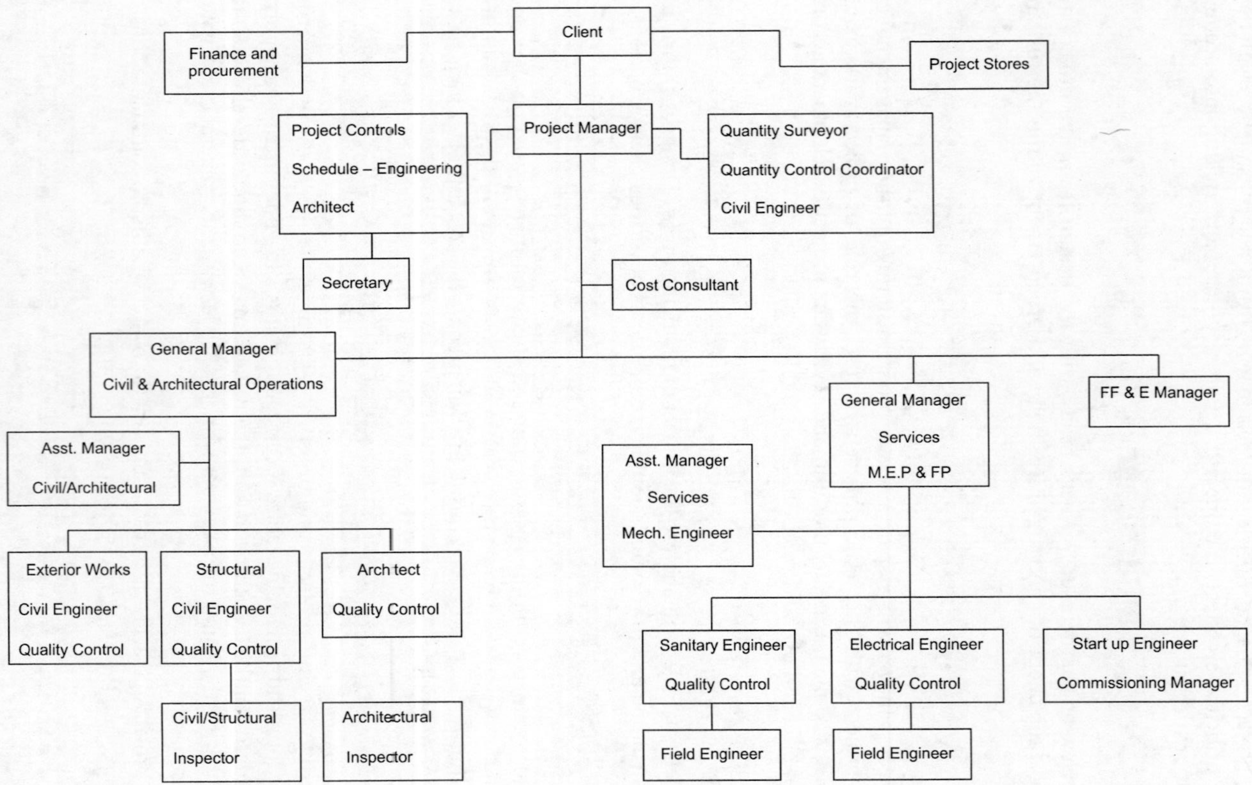

Fig. 1: Organigram project management

8.2 Staff buildup implementation will occur during the general construction tendering, including field staff and quality control team. The GMs will continue with the management and control of office/technical operations and with the additional responsibility of overseeing field staff performance. The quality control manager shall supervise and direct field staff activities and quality assurance programs outlined in Article III below. As field staff supervisor, the QC Manager shall report directly to the general managers in charge of civil-architectural-MEP operations. The additional staff will consist of structural inspectors, MEP inspectors and civil inspector as required. Responsibilities of each staff member will comprise:

8.2.1 General

(*a*) **All Staff Members** – Submit daily descriptions of construction activities occurring in respective member's area of responsibility. This data will be incorporated into a consolidated daily report prepared by the general managers.

(*b*) **All Field Staff Members** – Conduct preparatory, interim and final inspection of work being conducted within each respective area of responsibility.

(*c*) **All Field Staff Members** – Review contractor submittals for conformance with contract requirements and determine which submittal requires consultants' opinion.

(*d*) **GM – Civil/Architect & MEP** – Primary construction phase duties will pertain to the coordination of quality assurance monitoring activities conducted by members of the field staff. This includes:

(*i*) The collection, assembly and distribution of inspection reports.

(*ii*) Track progress of the contractor's work.

(*iii*) Review monthly invoices for correctness.

(*iv*) Provide field sketches, work plans and photographs for inclusion in monthly reports.

(*e*) **Field Inspection Engineers** -

(*i*) Monitor contractor's quality control programs and testing operations.

(*ii*) Collect and distribute testing reports.

(*iii*) Monitor progress of the work.

(*iv*) Assist and support general managers during the review of contractor invoices.

(*v*) Provide data and information required for the monthly report as required by the general manager.

Inspections are to be conducted by each member of the field staff to verify contractor compliance with contract documents. The inspections will be conducted in three stages – PREPARATORY, INTERIM AND FINAL. Written reports and punch lists are necessary for project distribution. These inspections will be performed in the following manner.

(*i*) **PREPARATORY** - Meet with the contractor providing work or materials for each specification. Verify that all submittals were received and authorized to proceed with the work which the consultant issued. Establish requirements for the construction of mock-ups required to gauge the level of quality expected. Verify that the contractor clearly understands security, sanitation, and safety requirements. Submit written report.

(*ii*) **INTERIM**- Perform periodic and daily inspections to verify that contractor is executing work according to contract documents and quality levels maintained. Monitor contractors' daily coordination meetings and respond to their queries. Produce lists of defective work and prepare directives in the form of an action notice informing the contract or of deviation from contract requirements.

(*iii*) **FINAL INSPECTIONS** – Upon contractor's notice of substantial completion of a designated portion of the project, perform inspections to:

1. verify if work has reached practical completion. "PUNCH LISTING" review of the work will commence, and
2. conduct a series of inspections to identify remaining work and defective work requiring the contractor's action.

In procuring capital goods from abroad, the sources have to be short-listed, offers received, and negotiated to get the best value for money. Government offers foreign exchange to import equipment from abroad on a reciprocal basis as the importing body does earn foreign exchange when operations commence. The Government takes a certain undertaking "ECGG" from the promoter in this regard. This also helps in getting the best bargain for tried and tested equipment.

Initial staff required during the design and tendering phases will consist of an office administrator/secretary, cost and scheduling controller, two general managers (C-A & MEP) and a quantity surveyor. The staff listed below is typically employed for a major 5-star hotel project of 400 to 600 rooms.

8.3 THE POSITION DESCRIPTION AND CORRESPONDING RESPONSIBILITIES

8.3.1 Office Administrator - Controller

(*a*) Setup & control the project file system, including finance, administrative and technical documents.

(*b*) Receive record and file project correspondence. Secretary to the office administrator will assist with processing and incorporating document control log data into the (MIS) Management Information System.

(*c*) Assist with maintaining registration logs for all correspondence, technical data & drawings.

(*d*) Assist with preparing daily and monthly reports based on input from technical staff.

(*e*) Control petty cash account and maintain transaction records.

(*f*) Assist with preparing invoices, letters and reports.

(*g*) Control phone and facsimile communications.

8.3.2 Cost-schedule – MIS Controller, Operator and MIS System Controller

(*a*) Oversee project financial operators, including cash flow monitoring/expediting invoice processing and owner procurement cost control;

(*b*) Oversee and update project master schedule and monitor contractor's construction critical path scheduling.

(*c*) Maintain management information system (MIS). Proficiency required in computer programs such as Primavera, project, Excel and Lotus. Maintain project MIS records and the duties include the following.

(*d*) Support general manager incharge of budget and scheduling.

(*e*) Produce data control documents, including spread sheets, flow charts and schedules. Monitor and track UHL procurement of estimates of owner purchased items.

(*f*) Assist with quantity survey document production and developing estimates and bills of quantities.

(*g*) Oversee project operations document control and information filing. Supervise the recording of MIS files in the Microsoft MIS program – Access, prepare and package budget and schedule data for monthly progress reports.

8.3.3 General Manager – Civil and Architectural

They oversee and monitor design, tender and construction activities with the secondary responsibility of supervising budget and cost control.

(*a*) **Design & Tender Phase:**

(*i*) Supervise the receiving, review and processing of civil and architectural technical documents.

(*ii*) Review design submittals for conformance with the design program, functional relationships, interdisciplinary coordination, code requirements, and constructability.

(*iii*) Review sub-consultants' design submittals for conformance with program requirements before transmittal for architectural consultant action.

(*b*) **Scheduling Assistance:** Prepare project work plans which will be used to monitor civil and architectural design and construction progress.

(*c*) **Cost and Budget Control:**

(*i*) Review and verify cost estimates and bills of quantities for accuracy and conformance with baseline budgets.

(*ii*) Oversee cost and budget control operations.

Specific duties include:

(*i*) Supervise the preparation of baseline project and construction budgets.

(*ii*) Review and monitor estimates provided by consultants.

(*iii*) Monitor contractor's cost estimates.

(*iv*) Supervise and review all architectural and civil consultants and contractor invoices. Provide recommendations for payment.

(*d*) **Construction Operations:**

(*i*) Oversee the performance of field staff. Supervise the collection of data required for daily and monthly reports and transmit to the project manager for review AMD publication.

(*ii*) Supervise the receiving and processing of civil/architectural technical documents (Office manager will assist with recording submittals in the document control logs).

(*iii*) Review contractor's submittals for conformance with design intent, coordination and code requirements and constructability.

(*iv*) Review civil/architectural contractor submittals for conformance with contract requirements before transmittal for consultant review.

(*v*) Oversee the performance of field staff. Supervise the collection of data required for daily and monthly reports and transmit to the office manager for publication.

8.3.4 General Manager - Mechanical, Electrical, Plumbing & Fire Protection

Will oversee and monitor design, tender and construction activities with secondary responsibilities for scheduling and control during the design and construction phase. Supervise the receiving review and processing of MEP technical documents produced by design consultants.

(*a*) **Design & Tender Phase:** Review MEP design submittals for conformance with the approved design program, appropriateness of plant space allocations and equipment adequacy. Oversee consultants' performance concerning interdisciplinary coordination, code requirement and constructability.

(*b*) **Scheduling Supervision:** Responsible for the monitoring of project scheduling. Review of schedules submitted by all design consultants and contractors. Develop project work plans and schedules with the assistance of the GM in charge of civil and architectural operations with the support of the scheduling supervisor.

(*c*) **Cost control Assistance:** Assist the general manager responsible for cost control and budget analysis with reviewing and analyzing budget data and estimates submitted by MEP design consultants and contractors. Review and verify MEP cost estimates and bills of quantities for accuracy and conformance with baseline budgets.

(*d*) **Construction Operation:** Oversee the performance of MEP field staff. Supervise the collection of data required for daily and monthly reports and transmit to the office manager for publication.

(*i*) Supervise the receiving, review and processing of all MEP and FP technical documents.

(*ii*) Review MEP contractor submittals for conformance with design intent, coordination, code requirements, and constructability.

(*iii*) Review MEP contractor submittals for conformance with contract requirements before Transmittal for consultant review.

(*iv*) Oversee the review of construction schedules and prepare work plans which will be used to monitor the construction process.

(*v*) Review and verify contractor cost estimates and bills of quantities for accuracy.

8.3.5 Quality Control/Quantity Survey Operations

Will be responsible for monitoring design consultants' cost estimates, project budget and contractors' bills of quantities in support of the general manager in charge of budget control. As quality control supervisor, monitor and coordinate quality assurance programs during the design and construction phases.

(*i*) **QS** – Responsibilities include preparing budget control spread sheets, material take-off and unit cost evaluations during construction operations, and verifying quantities and quality of materials in accordance with the requirements of the construction contract. Initial primary duties include the monitoring of excavation and utilities installations.

(*ii*) **QC** – Responsibilities include coordinating interim inspections, final inspections and "Punch Listing" activities. Support the general managers in conducting preparatory inspections.

(*iii*) Maintain construction progress records and daily reports.

9.0 PROJECT PROCEDURE MANUAL

Project procedure manual should be prepared in consultation with the consultants. The project manager will prepare a project procedure manual that covers the following:

(*a*) Project details
(*b*) Directory
(*c*) Communication
(*d*) Reporting
(*e*) Financial matters
(*f*) Meetings
(*g*) Drawings
(*h*) Circulation of correspondences
(*i*) Bid packages
(*j*) Tenders
(*k*) Payments
(*l*) Defect liability
(*m*) Certifications
(*n*) Insurance
(*o*) Statutory requirements

10.0 DESIGN TEAM SELECTION REQUIREMENTS

The owner, assisted by the project manager, will define the design team:

(*a*) Design scope
(*b*) Pre-qualification
(*c*) Procedure to follow
(*d*) Coordination
(*e*) Advice on special studies and review
(*f*) Drawing details and delivery

The design team selected at this stage comprises M.E.P. consultants, interior and landscape designers.

11.0 CONSTRUCTION STRATEGY

The project manager will ensure that all aspects of development are covered and will advise the staff on site management (see Chapter: 08), including phasing requirements, logistics, safety and security and industrial relations, quality control, environmental impact planning and handing over sequence.

12.0 MASTER PROJECT SCHEDULE

The project manager will prepare the master project schedule, which will form a part of the contract documents, another master schedule trade-wise, indicating the commencement and completion of each activity and update the same while monitoring. Refer Fig. 2: General Construction Project Schedule (Bar Chart) and Fig. 3A & 3B: Master Project Schedule – A Case study.

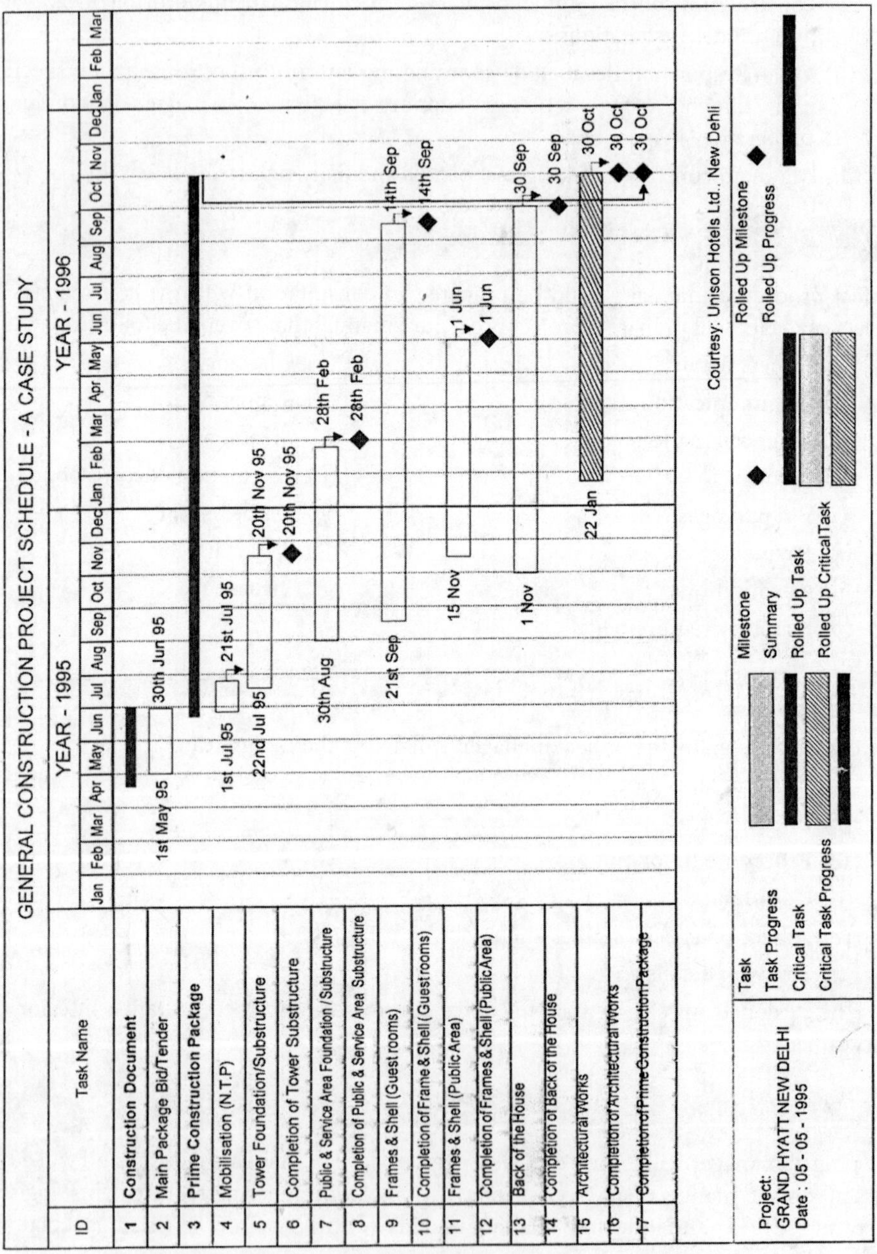

Fig. 2: General construction project schedule (bar chart)

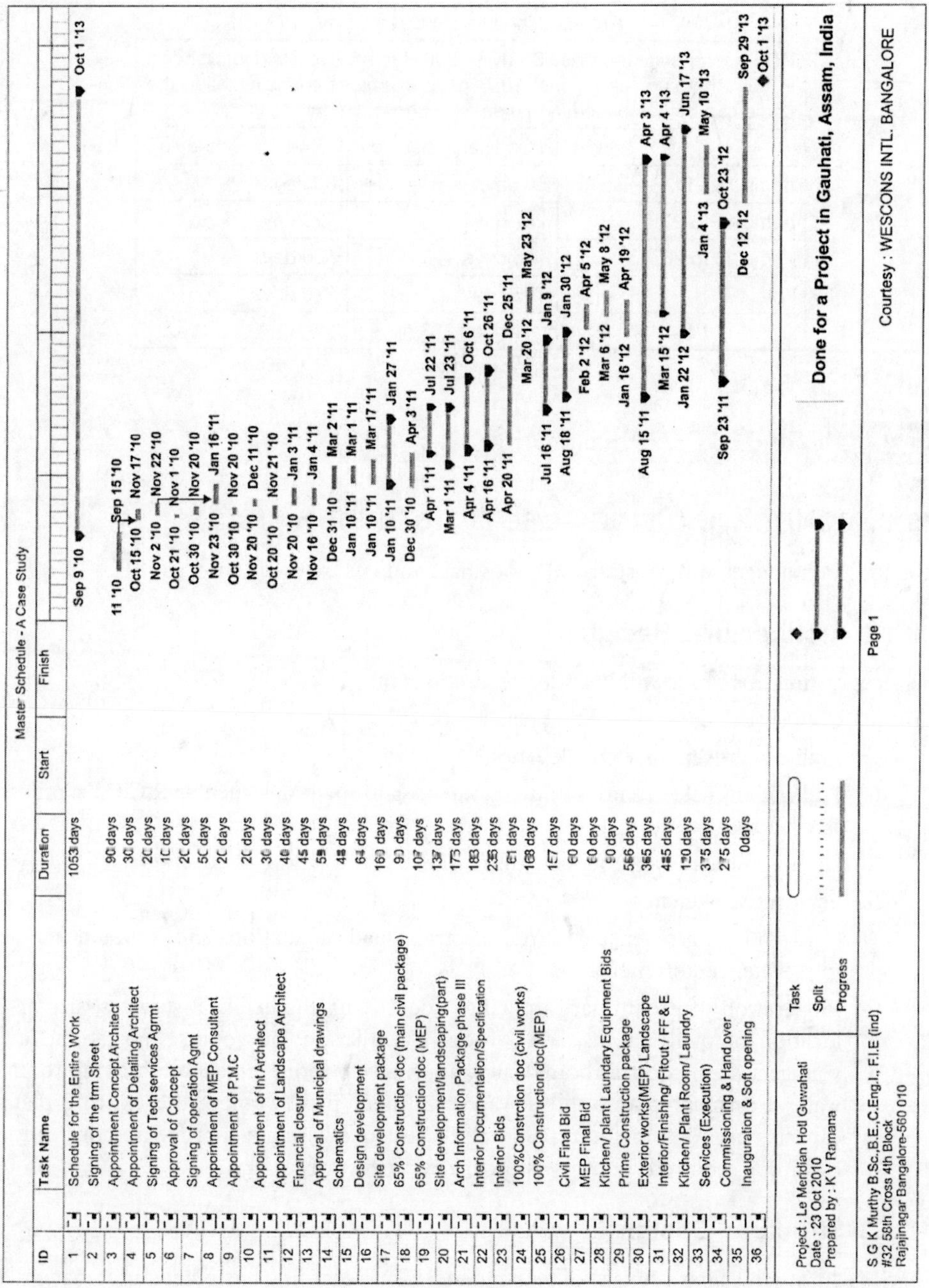
Master Schedule - A Case Study
ID
Task Name
Duration
Start
Finish
1 Schedule for the Entire Work 1053 days Sep 9 '10 Oct 1 '13
2 Signing of the trm Sheet
3 Appointment Concept Architect 90 days 11 '10 Sep 15 '10
4 Appointment of Detailing Architect 30 days Oct 15 '10 Nov 17 '10
5 Signing of Tech services Agrmt 20 days Nov 2 '10 Nov 22 '10
6 Approval of Concept 10 days Oct 21 '10 Nov 1 '10
7 Signing of operation Agmt 20 days Oct 30 '10 Nov 20 '10
8 Appointment of MEP Consultant 50 days Nov 23 '10 Jan 16 '11
9 Appointment of P.M.C 20 days Oct 30 '10 Nov 20 '10
10 Appointment of Int Architect 20 days Nov 20 '10 Dec 11 '10
11 Appointment of Landscape Architect 30 days Oct 20 '10 Nov 21 '10
12 Financial closure 40 days Nov 20 '10 Jan 3 '11
13 Approval of Municipal drawings Nov 16 '10 Jan 4 '11
14 Schematics Dec 31 '10 Mar 2 '11
15 Design development 48 days Jan 10 '11 Mar 1 '11
16 Site development package 64 days Jan 10 '11 Mar 17 '11
17 65% Construction doc (main civil package) Jan 10 '11 Jan 27 '11
18 65% Construction doc (MEP) Dec 30 '10 Apr 3 '11
19 Site development/landscaping(part) 107 days Apr 1 '11 Jul 22 '11
20 Arch Information Package phase III 137 days Mar 1 '11 Jul 23 '11
21 Interior Documentation/Specification 175 days Apr 4 '11 Oct 6 '11
22 Interior Bids 183 days Apr 16 '11 Oct 26 '11
23 100%Constrction doc (civil works) 235 days Apr 20 '11 Dec 25 '11
24 100% Construction doc(MEP) 61 days Mar 20 '12 May 23 '12
25 Civil Final Bid 168 days Jul 16 '11 Jan 9 '12
26 MEP Final Bid 157 days Aug 18 '11 Jan 30 '12
27 Kitchen/ plant Laundary Equipment Bids 60 days Feb 2 '12 Apr 5 '12
28 Prime Construction package 60 days Mar 6 '12 May 8 '12
29 Exterior works(MEP) Landscape 90 days Jan 16 '12 Apr 19 '12
30 Interior/Finishing/ Fitout / FF & E 566 days Aug 15 '11 Apr 3 '13
31 Kitchen/ Plant Room/ Laundry Mar 15 '12 Apr 4 '13
32 Services (Execution) 365 days Jan 22 '12 Jun 17 '13
33 Commissioning & Hand over Jan 4 '13 May 10 '13
34 Inauguration & Soft opening 120 days Sep 23 '11 Oct 23 '12
35 375 days Dec 12 '12 Sep 29 '13
36 275 days Oct 1 '13
0days
Project : Le Meridian Hotl Guwahati
Date : 23 Oct 2010
Prepared by : K V Ramana
Task
Split
Progress
Done for a Project in Gauhati, Assam, India
S G K Murthy B.Sc.,B.E.,C.Eng.I., F.I.E (ind)
#32 58th Cross 4th Block
Rajajinagar Bangalore-560 010
Page 1
Courtesy : WESCONS INTL. BANGALORE

Fig. 3A:

Project Schedule – A Case Study

With reference to the Case Study for 200 Rooms Five Star Hotel shown in this Annexure as against 1053 days estimated for completion the same can be completed in 670 days as shown below:		
	Original Schedule	Present Schedule
Items 1 to 14	50 days	30 days
Items 15 to 22	287 days	120 days
Items 23 to 26	716 days	520 days
Total	1053 days	670 days
Total saving 383 days		

Fig. 3B:

13.0 DESIGN COORDINATION

13.1 CONCEPTUAL AND SCHEMATIC DESIGN PHASE

The Project manager and his staff will coordinate and ensure the following:

13.1.1 Architectural Design

Services during this phase will include preparations of:

(*a*) Conceptual site and building plans.

(*b*) Preliminary sections and elevations

(*c*) Preliminary selection of building systems and materials such as R.C.C., stainless steel and bricks, etc.

(*d*) Developments of approximate dimensions.

(*e*) Perspective sketches.

(*f*) Carry out comprehensive HVAC, electrical load calculations and computation for total water requirement.

(*g*) Preparation of preliminary drawings, identifying the external services, size and location of plant rooms, AHU rooms, ventilation fan rooms; substation; low voltage system control room; water tanks, pump room, fire fighting pump room, water treatment plant, and sewage treatment plant (unless the existing plant capacity permits) including holding discussions with appropriate authorities for obtaining required statutory approvals whenever necessary.

13.1.2 Structural Design

Services during this phase consist of recommendations regarding basic structural materials and systems, analyses and development of conceptual design solutions for a pre-determined structural system and alternative structural systems. Unless otherwise indicated by the owner and operator, the consultants will follow the prevalent codes.

13.1.3 Civil Design

Services during this phase will consist of the analysis of alternative materials and systems and development of conceptual designs for:

- On-site utility systems
- Fire fighting and suppression
- Paving (Landscape design)
- Off-site utilities work
- Drainage systems

13.1.4 Landscape Design

This phase includes consideration of alternative materials, systems and equipment development of conceptual design solutions for landforms, lawns and plantings based on program requirements, physical site characteristics, design objectives and environmental requirements. This work will be carried out in close conjunction with the architectural design undertaken by the chosen landscape architect. A 3D model will be prepared using data digitized from the topographical map prepared during the site survey. This digital computer model will allow the optimal balance of project earthworks during the conceptual landscape design.

13.1.5 Interior Design

Services during this phase will include preparation of space allocation and utilization plans based on functional relationships, consideration of alternative materials, systems and equipment and development of conceptual design solutions for architectural, mechanical, electrical and equipment requirements to establish partition locations, furniture and equipment locations.

13.1.6 Preliminary Cost Estimate

Based on schematic studies and design work described above, the consultant will prepare a preliminary cost estimate broken down into components described. This estimate of the probable construction cost will include the provision for contingencies. Q.S will be responsible for determining unit rates for all local construction items and equipment costs, while the architect will be responsible for costing all imported items and equipment.

13.1.7 Project Schedule

Based on the studies and designs prepared during this phase, the consultant will update the project schedule. This schedule will consider the proposed method of contracting for the project and will look at minimizing the project implementation period. The schedule will assume a timely review and approval process by the owner and operator (use of project management software such as Primavera, Microsoft project or any new user-friendly software is suggested). The consultant will provide a specified number of full sets of the preliminary design documents to the owner once approved and hand over a set to the operator.

13.1.8 Detailed Design and Cost Estimate

The project manager will ensure that the work will be undertaken in two phases:

(*a*) The design development phase

(*b*) The construction documents phase

Utilizing the approved preliminary design documents, the consultant will complete these design development and construction document phases within a predetermined time frame. Work undertaken during this phase will include the following elements:

13.2 DESIGN DEVELOPMENT PHASE

13.2.1 Architectural Design

Continuing from the schematic design, the final scope, relationships, forms, size and appearance of the project will be established through:

(*a*) Plans, sections and elevations.
(*b*) Typical construction details.
(*c*) 3D sketches.
(*d*) Study model.
(*e*) Final material selections.
(*f*) Equipment layouts.

13.2.2 Structural Design

The structural systems analyzed during the schematic design phase will be developed in sufficient detail to establish:

(*a*) Foundation design.
(*b*) Basic and final structural dimension criteria.
(*c*) Preliminary sizing of major structural components.
(*d*) Critical coordination clearances.
(*e*) Outline specifications.

Prepare detailed design and tender drawings, including layout drawings incorporating all services elements as given in the scope of work 1.0. The consultant agrees that the designs are subject to prior review by the owner at his discretion.

13.2.3 Civil Design

Building on the work completed for the schematic design, the consultant will establish the final scope and preliminary details for on-site and off-site civil works. Outline specifications and materials lists will also be prepared.

13.2.4 Landscape Design

Work under this phase includes the development of outline specifications to establish the final scope and preliminary details for landscape work.

13.2.5 Interior Design

Work under this phase includes the development of outline specifications to establish final scope and preliminary details relative to:

(*a*) Interior construction of the project.
(*b*) Special Interior design features.
(*c*) Furniture, furnishings and equipment selections.
(*d*) Materials and finishes and colors.

13.2.6 Specifications

In addition to the outline specifications developed as described above, the consultant will prepare the following information for review by the owner and the operator:

(*a*) Draft general and supplementary conditions of the contract for construction.

(*b*) Outline specifications and brief for identifying significant materials, systems and equipment and their criteria and quality standards.

13.2.7 Cost Estimate

At this stage, the consultant will revise the estimate of the probable construction cost taking into consideration:

(*a*) Availability of materials and labor.

(*b*) Project delivery procedures

(*c*) Construction sequencing and scheduling.

(*d*) Changes in the scope of the project.

(*e*) Adjustments in quality standards.

13.2.8 Project Schedule

At this stage, the project schedule will be updated.

13.3 CONSTRUCTION DOCUMENT PHASE

During this phase, the project manager will ensure that the detailed design drawings, specifications, bill of quantities and cost estimate are prepared. This includes:

13.3.1 Discipline Coordination

The consultant will coordinate the work between the architectural, engineering and other involved disciplines. The architect will undertake this coordination role. In addition, all documents will be reviewed and checked before submission to the Owner.

13.3.2 Architectural Design

This work consists of preparing drawings based on the approved design development documents. The drawings set forth, in detail, the architectural construction requirements for the hotel. Architectural drawings will be provided in the following categories: Index, Symbols, Abbreviations, Notes, Location map, Site plan, Temporary work, Plans, Room material schedule, Door schedule, Key drawings, Sections, Exterior elevations, Detailed floor plans, Interior elevations, Reflected ceiling plans, Vertical circulation, Stairs, Elevators, Exterior details and Interior details.

13.3.3 Structural Design

This work consists of the preparation of final structural engineering calculations, drawings and specifications based on the approved design development documents. This sets out, in detail, the structural construction requirements for the hotel. Structural drawings will be divided into the following categories: General notes, Site work, Framing plans, Elevations, Schedules, Concrete, Masonry, Structural steel, Timber and Special design.

13.3.4 Civil Design

This work consists of final civil engineering calculations, drawings and specifications based on the approved design development documents. It sets out, in detail, the civil construction requirements for the hotel. Designs for access roads, parking areas and drains will be carried out using suitable software.

13.3.5 Landscape Design

This work consists of preparing drawings and specifications based on the approved design development documents. This sets out, in detail, the landscape requirements for the project. This work will be undertaken utilizing any suitable software to balance earth works as part of the design process.

13.3.6 Interior Design

This work consists of preparing drawings, specifications and furnishings, furniture and equipment schedules based on the approved design development documents. This sets out, in detail, the requirements for interior construction and furniture, furnishings and equipment for the Hotel. i.e., F.F. & E.

13.3.7 Specifications

The consultant will prepare a complete set of technical specifications for the hotel, which will describe materials, systems and equipment, workmanship, quality and performance criteria required for the construction of the hotel.

13.3.8 Cost Estimate

Once the construction documents are complete, the consultant will prepare a detailed cost estimate for the hotel. This will be based on a detailed bill of quantities which will be broken down into standard work items. The quantity take-off work will be the responsibility of each designer and will be coordinated by a cost engineer. The local architect will calculate unit rates for each construction work item based on his experience with the local construction market.

14.0 COST PLANNING AND BUDGETING

The stage-wise cost planning and course corrections are essential to ensure no cost overruns. The estimate at the concept stage, at the tender stage, and after receiving tenders will provide the necessary basis for adjustments and deviations, if any, before placing a work order. When the design development to the required degree of quantity and specifications are available, a detailed cost estimate is arrived at, which when agreed with the client becomes the project cost. Cost reporting formats and cash flow analysis will enable review and monitoring of the project budget.

Please see Section 8.3.2 for "Cost-Schedule - MIS Controller, Operator and Management Information System Controller" and "Annexure:03 – Costing of 5-Star Hotels & Resorts".

15.0 STATUTORY APPROVALS

The project manager should work out a mechanism to obtain statutory approvals from different agencies of the government. One must establish liaisons with the authorities to monitor statutory approvals regarding building regulations, water supply, gas, electricity and transportation (See Annexure:08 - List of Statutory & Local body approvals).

16.0 SHORTLISTING OF CONSTRUCTION AGENCIES AND MATERIAL SUPPLIERS

16.1 PRE-CONSTRUCTION ACTIVITIES

Following review and acceptance of the final report, the following traditional pre-construction activities will be carried out. An alternative approach involving earlier pre-construction is described as follows:

16.2 PRE-QUALIFICATION OF CONTRACTORS

A pre-qualification document will be prepared to identify qualified contractors. The pre-qualification questionnaire will request information on each firm's financial status, personnel, experience, as well as details of plant and equipment.

Pre-qualification criteria will be developed and used to identify firms for tendering. The minimum requirements will be based on the company's size, experience, billings, performance and other factors. The project manager proposes limiting the choice to international contractors with local expertise. The list of pre-qualified firms will be submitted to the owner for their review and concurrence.

16.3 PREPARATION OF CONTRACT DOCUMENTS

Development of the contract documents will begin with preparing the detailed tender documents. These will be based on the construction documents and will include:

(*a*) Description of works
(*b*) Engineering and architectural drawings
(*c*) Specifications
(*d*) Procedures and schedule of construction
(*e*) Cost estimate and
(*f*) Contract clauses

Other documents that will be prepared as part of the complete contract package include:

(*a*) Invitation to tender
(*b*) Instructions to tenderers
(*c*) Form of tender
(*d*) Schedule to major plant and equipment
(*e*) Schedule of offices, workshops and stores
(*f*) Schedule of senior staff
(*g*) Schedule of proposed sub-contractors
(*h*) Declaration of foreign exchange requirements, if any
(*i*) Declaration of no exception to tender
(*j*) Conditions of contract.

The concerned project manager will submit the complete contract package to the owner for review.

16.4.0 Tendering of Contract

The following procedures will be used for tendering the contract:

16.4.1 Prepare and Distribute Pre-qualification Notice

Before the publication of the pre-qualification notice, the format of the notice and pre-qualification forms will be drafted and submitted to the owner for approval. The notice will then be distributed to appropriate publications on behalf of the owner. The project manager will answer any queries of the owner; provide copies of all queries and responses.

16.4.2 Analyze Pre-qualification Submissions

The project manager and representative will analyze all pre-qualification submittals and prepare a report summarizing the evaluation and providing recommendations for a contractor short list.

(*a*) Pre-qualification submissions should consist of the contractor's "Bench mark" as well as the contractor's track record of completed works of similar nature, volume and year of completion

(*b*) Staff available to be posted on the job with their qualification and experience

(*c*) Financial backing and testimonials, if any.

16.4.3 Notify Contractors and Distribute Bid Documents

The project manager will notify short listed contractors and distribute the bid documents

16.4.4 Hold Pre Bid Conference

The project manager will prepare for and conduct a pre-bid conference with the site officer. They will answer questions of the contractor during the conference and project site inspection. The project will be explained, and important project components will be shown to contractors' representatives.

Following the pre-bid conference, all contractors' queries will be collated, and all responses will be fully discussed with the owner before the written response. A report including all queries and responses made during the conference and site visit will be prepared and submitted for review.

16.4.5 Evaluation of Tenders

The project manager and respective consultants will evaluate each tender and provide a report summarizing the following:

(*a*) Analysis of unit rates.

(*b*) Analysis of contractor foreign/local currency requirements and overall construction cost.

(*c*) All forms, bills of quantities, and various schedules complete and in order with correct computations.

(*d*) Technical and cost impact of any proposed alternatives.

(*e*) Points requiring further discussion with each tenderer.

(*f*) Issues that have arisen and recommendations for appropriate action.

(*g*) Recommendation on post-tender communications required with each tenderer, not in full compliance.

(*h*) Results and any post-tender communications.

The report will contain the project manager and consultants' recommendations for contractor selection.

16.4.6 Assistance in Negotiation

If requested, the project manager will make available an experienced contract engineer to assist the project manager in formulating the contractor - owner agreement.

16.4.7 Alternative Pre-Qualification and Contracting Approach

One of the major concerns in luxury hotel construction is quality control assurance, given the numerous traders and crafts involved in the construction. Cost overruns and duplication of work sometimes occur due to a lack of contractor coordination.

A possible solution to this problem is to involve the contractor during the design phase to ensure the development of the most efficient and economical designs and construction programs.

To facilitate this, pre-qualification of contractors would occur during the initial months of the project. A shortlist would be developed, and a contractor selected based on negotiations with the top two or three firms. This work method would alter the work sequence slightly, but the overall time schedule and other contracting features would not change.

17.0 CONSTRUCTION PHASE

17.1 SITE SUPERVISION AND COORDINATION

Construction supervision is a complex set of tasks requiring a high level of skill and attention by the project manager, who must be responsive to the continuing flow of inquiries, submittals and requests for changes and payments that characterize daily construction contract administration. Construction supervision includes those activities which provide direction and overall control of the construction effort and the entire field supervision effort, which assures quality construction, contractor compliance with all plans and specifications and on-time performance.

The field supervision effort requires an extensive inspection apparatus, prompt decision making at the job level, thorough documentation, and responsive action to support management's need for prompt and accurate cost and schedule information.

There are generally four keys to the success of the project manager's construction supervision approach.

(*a*) **Design and contracts:** The first key is the importance of good designs and good contracts. This approach emphasizes both aspects, as discussed in the above sections. No construction supervision techniques can completely overcome the obstacle of design errors or weaknesses in contract provisions.

(*b*) **Management approach:** The second key is a sound management approach, supported by a powerful Management Information System (MIS). Most construction management challenges arise from coordination issues between contracts. The MIS helps minimize these problems. In addition, MIS provides helpful information for project cost and schedule control. Logs of submittals and other documents are stored and well managed for easy tracking and retrieval. The Project Manager's MIS and management approach have been developed and proven on large construction projects worldwide.

(*c*) **Uniform standards:** The third key is the establishment of comprehensive and uniform standards and procedures for construction supervision. The project manager's proposal presents the detailed procedures it has used with success worldwide.

(*d*) **Qualified staff:** The fourth key to construction management is qualified staff. The staff should be highly experienced in large construction projects worldwide.

The pre-construction/procurement bidding strategy needs planning of detailed guidelines, soliciting, interpreting, and assisting in developing bid lists, prequalifying contractors and trade schedules, and attending bid clarification meetings.

17.2 SUBMITTALS AND APPROVALS

All construction projects require the production, transmittal and control of a wide range of documents and data, including shop drawings, product data, samples, mock-ups, test results, warranties, maintenance agreements, bonds, project photographs, record drawings, field measurement data, operating and maintenance manuals. Under the terms of the contract, the general contractor and sub-contractors involved in the project will be required to submit such material for review and approval.

The discussion and task descriptions below focus on shop drawings but apply to all contractor submittals.

Responsibilities and procedures for processing contractor submittals are typically defined in the general conditions of the contract and by local trade practices. These procedures will be modified and adjusted to meet the specific requirements of the project delivery system for the project.

When the delivery approach is based on design-award-build, the shop drawing process is sequential, performed after the contract documents are completed and after construction has begun. The general contractor must prepare the shop drawings, review, and approve them before they are forwarded to the project manager or owner.

In fast-track projects, shop drawings for one portion of the work may be developed before construction documents on other parts are completed. Moreover, shop drawings may be made based on design development (or even schematic design) drawings. Together with the pressure of time inherent with fast-track documents production, these conditions increase the problems associated with coordination. These problems are further complicated in CM managed projects, where the CM might not have the responsibility to construct the project according to the contract documents. Individual sub-contractors are obligated to produce various portions of the work, and there is no clear assignment of overall responsibility. This increases the importance of careful coordination during the review of shop drawings.

17.3 PROCESSING AND APPROVAL PROCEDURES

The process of reviewing and approving shop drawings operates best if all participants – contractors, project manager and owner know in advance what they are expected to do according to the contract. The following list provides an overview of administrative procedures that the project manager will implement to ensure the timely review and approval of shop drawings and other submittals.

(*a*) Office and field personnel shall follow the provisions related to shop drawings contained in the general conditions of the contract.

(*b*) During the pre-construction conference, the specific contract requirements concerning the processing of shop drawings and other submittals will be reviewed. Contractors will be required to adhere to their contractual obligations to check and approve shop drawings before submitting them for approval throughout the project.

(*c*) Review of shop drawings shall be confined to determining whether they conform to the design concept and the requirements of the contract documents. Approval does not extend to information not called for in the contract documents.

(*d*) Shop drawings and other submittals that have been submitted without being checked and approved by the contractor will not be accepted.

(*e*) Shop drawings and other submittals shall not be accepted from anyone other than the contractor.

(*f*) A shop drawing and other submittal logs will be established and maintained in the office to record the dates on which all submittals were received and returned.

(*g*) If contractor submittals cannot be approved, written documentation will be provided explaining why they have been rejected or returned without approvals.

(*h*) A shop drawing or other submittal approval stamp shall be used, indicating approval for conformance with the design concept and the information in the contract documents.

17.4 CONTRACTOR'S APPROVAL AND SUBMISSION

As indicated above, contractor reviews of the shop drawings and other submittals before transmittal to the project manager and owner are mandatory. To facilitate review of shop drawings and other submittals, the contractor's review and approval should include field dimensions and construction criteria and written notation regarding any information in the shop drawings that do not conform to the contract documents. The stringent implementation of these procedures ensures that the contractor does not use the project manager to provide the initial review of submittals from their sub-contractors.

17.5 REVIEW AND APPROVAL OF SHOP DRAWINGS

A consistent standard for the processing and approval of shop drawings and other submittals will be established by the project manager.

(*a*) Upon receipt, shop drawings and other submittals will be dated, stamped and given an appropriate identifying number.

(*b*) Since the process of receiving, examining, approving and distributing shop drawings is a complicated one, a schedule showing the progress of these drawings in the office of the project manager will aid orderly processing and enable any delays in approval to be tracked and accounted for.

(*c*) Procedures for handling shop drawings between the project manager and owner will be carefully scheduled and maintained.

17.6 FIELD/SITE ADMINISTRATION

The main concern and duty of the project manager are whether or not the construction is proceeding as per the contract documents. The temptation to become involved in the construction process itself can be avoided. Effective construction supervision and coordination are critical factors in successfully completing a complex construction project. It is also established on a detailed understanding of the contracts between the various parties and effective "contractor relations".

17.7 UNDERSTANDING OF THE CONTRACTS

The duties and responsibilities of the various parties to the construction contract shall be as defined by the various contracts for the work. A complete and thorough understanding of these contracts is essential to the efficiency of the project manager on the project.

17.8 CONTRACTOR RELATIONS

Effective construction supervision incorporates some understanding of the contractor's problems. The project manager must be exacting in requirements but not so strict and inflexible as to be unreasonable. In some circumstances, minor modifications may be permitted to accommodate field conditions without affecting the design. Typically while the project manager, with the owner's consent, interprets any specifications by the drawings, he has neither the power nor the authority to modify or waive any provision of the contract.

The project manager should have established "Rules of Conduct" for the construction supervision, which serves to prevent it from undermining the authority and responsibilities of the contractor. Such rules include:

(*a*) Unless specifically required under the contract, the project manager will not attempt to dictate or direct construction means, methods, techniques, sequences, and procedures. If the consultant is not satisfied that the contractor's procedure will produce the intended result, the project manger will discuss the matter with the owner.

(*b*) The project manager shall not give instructions to the contractor's employees. If the work is not being appropriately performed, the project manager will inform the contractor's superintendent to take corrective action.

(*c*) All information imparted and decisions made as a result of communications made directly with the suppliers and sub-contractors shall be confirmed with the prime contractor.

17.9 CLERICAL DUTIES

Effective clerical procedures will be of prime importance to the effective conduct of the project.

The project manager will establish a system of documents control that will enable the processing and tracking of all materials submitted and generated as part of the execution of the project. Field office files shall be kept up-to-date and maintained for ready reference at the job site during the entire construction period. Files will include:

(*a*) A current and complete set of all contract documents.

(*b*) Project correspondence sent to the project manager filed according to office standards.

(*c*) Proposal requests, supplemental instructions filed according to office standards.

(*d*) Proposal requests, supplemental instructions, change orders, and construction change authorizations, including any interpretive documents.

(*e*) Shop drawing, product data and log.

(*f*) All approved samples will be kept at the job site as a basis for comparison and should be appropriately tagged and logged.

(*g*) Copies of all requisitions for payment made by the contractor.

(*h*) Any other reports related to the project.

17.10 DAILY LOG

The project manager's site staff will keep a daily log covering the important events at the project site. This log constitutes a convenient chronological record of the project and can be extremely important in settling disputes. The daily log will record the following information.

(*a*) Weather and ground conditions.

(*b*) Work performed, including the starting and completion of any unit of work.

(*c*) Construction difficulties encountered and remedial measures employed.

(*d*) Record of significant delays together with cause.

(*e*) Materials and equipment delivered to project site.

18.0 BUILDABILITY ADVICE AND VALUE ENGINEERING

Optimize construction techniques with time, cost and quality considerations. Monitor design as it evolves and advise value engineering opportunities worthy of further evaluation of the project by undertaking value engineering studies.

19.0 RISK ANALYSIS OF MANAGEMENT

Foresee risk elements and render timely advice to the client to avoid impeding or in built danger, if any. The design team may overlook or ignore some important factors while designing, and it may result in unforeseen structural failures causing the loss of many lives and property. Insurance provisions must be taken only as a last resort and not a risk-covering strategy.

20.0 REVIEW, ANALYSIS AND MONITORING OF CONTRACTOR'S WORK PROGRAMME

Review and analyze the contractor's program and procedures to determine the accuracy of cash flow projections, operational efficiency and safety of construction operations, manpower and staffing strategy. Determine areas where additional planning is required and make recommendations to the contractor for improvement.

20.1 REVIEW ANALYSIS WITH THE EMPLOYER AND ORGANISE AND CONDUCT A PRE-CONSTRUCTION MEETING THAT WILL

(*a*) Delineate the organization and lines of authority of the employer and the entire project team.

(*b*) Review the terms and conditions of the construction contracts and impress upon the contractors the client's intent to enforce all contract requirements.

(*c*) Review all standard reporting forms to be used on the project.

(*d*) Discuss insurance and bonding requirements to ensure compliance with the conditions of the construction contract.

(*e*) Establish requirements for shop drawing submittal review.

(*f*) Discuss procedures for procurement expediting.

20.2 PROGRAMME CONTROL

20.2.1 Master Program Review

(*a*) Periodically update a project design and construction program. The program shall be reviewed with the employer, consultants and contractors at predetermined milestone dates agreed with the employer.

(*b*) Provide a master program for the management of consultants and contractors on the project, including activity sequences, durations, and the employer's occupancy requirements showing portions of the project having occupancy priority. The master program is for comparative purposes and may be adjusted to reflect the project manager's assessment of the consultants and contractors programs.

(*c*) Provide regular monitoring of the consultant's and contractor's detailed program as the project progresses. Identify potential variances between programs and probable completion dates. Discuss with the employer, consultants and contractors adjustments in the program to meet the likely completion date. Provide summary reports that monitor and document changes in program. The master program and its accomplishments shall be included in the monthly report to the Employer.

20.2.2 Review of Contractor's Construction Program

(*a*) Review the contractor's network of activities, addressing the validity of logic, missing activities, activity durations, location indicators on the site and designation of responsibilities, manpower allocation, and costs associated with each design and construction activity.

(*b*) Examine contractor mobilization program to ensure that equipment and materials required early in the construction phase are available.

(*c*) Recommend to the contractors changes in the sequence of activities to increase operating efficiency.

(*d*) Ensure that the required time and cost resources are allocated to each program activity.

(*e*) Ensure that the contractor complies with the contractual obligations relative to program preparation and submittal.

20.2.3 Monitoring the Contractor's Program

(*a*) Review each program revision with the contractors to confirm compliance with the master program approved by the employer, and address the immediate problems resulting from logic changes.

(*b*) Identify potential conflicts of activities due to delays of certain activities.

(*c*) Review the cost assigned to each activity as the program progresses to ensure cash flow requirements are not altered.

(*d*) Examine the contractor procurement and inventory system for missing items, lead items and areas of potential delays.

(*e*) Review the contractor's program regularly. Updates will be evaluated for accuracy. The impact on the overall project program will be examined.

21.0 MANAGEMENT OF CONSTRUCTION

(*a*) Advise the employer on the issues relating to financial and operational procedures of the contractor.

(*b*) Provide detailed and organized documentation of all activities of the entire project team. Records will be made available to the Employer to ensure compliance with all contractual obligations.

(*c*) Consult with the Employer's legal representatives on questions of interpretation of the conditions of contracts.

(*d*) Monitor the contractor's operations and review required submittal to ensure compliance with all terms and conditions of the contract.

(*e*) Implement procedures for variation orders, site instructions, program review, progress payments, contractor claims, on-site safety, site security, procurement review, reports information exchange, and compute operations.

(*f*) Establish a comprehensive project library. Records and copies of all correspondence, reports, and other documentation should be cataloged and filed.

(*g*) Ensure that all required test data, operating manuals and maintenance information are submitted in an organized form.

(*h*) Establish procedures for producing and maintaining current sets of built drawings.

(*i*) Discuss with the consultants' contractor's requests for interpretation of the meaning and intent of drawings and specifications, and assist in the resolution of any questions which may arise.

(*j*) In collaboration with the consultant, establish and implement procedures for expediting the processing and approval of shop drawings and samples without assuming any responsibility for the content or results of said documents.

(*k*) In collaboration with the consultants, establish and implement procedures for determining and certifying practical and final completion.

21.1 QUALITY CONTROL OF CONSTRUCTION

(*a*) Review installation procedures to ensure that materials and equipment are correctly handled, detailing, and connections are as specified.

(*b*) Work with the contractor to develop an understanding of the contractor's inspection programs; develop special procedures for inspecting work and taking necessary corrective actions before authorizing monthly progress payments.

(*c*) Examine procedures for procurement and handling of construction materials and equipment.

(*d*) Review contractor's plans for installation and testing of equipment.

(*e*) Receive and monitor contractor's and consultants' detailed punch lists for all project areas when substantially complete.

(*f*) Develop a comprehensive program for the completion of punch list items before acceptance.

(*g*) Clarify warranty and maintenance requirements and ensure that the employer and the contractor agree on procedures to be followed during the warranty period.

(*h*) Ensure that the contractor complies with all terms and conditions of the contracts to the fullest extent before final payment is made and retainage released.

21.2 COST CONTROL

21.2.1 Project Budget

(*a*) Review and analyze the consultant's construction estimate. Establish a project budget for those areas under the project manager's responsibility for the employer's approval as soon as major project requirements have been identified.

(*b*) Develop and implement a budget tracking system. Review, analyze, and update the budget, including variation orders, for approval by the employer at predetermined milestone dates. Advice the employer and architect, or other consultants, if it appears that the project budget may not be met.

21.3 CONTRACTORS PROGRESS PAYMENTS

(*a*) Analyze the billing projections prepared by the contractor; review, confirm the monthly quantities of work in place; and review all supporting documentation prepared by the contractors.

(*b*) Compare the payment requested with the costs assigned to that month's program activities, and in association with the consultants, make payment recommendations (certifications) to the employer.

21.4 PROJECT COST TRACKING:

(*a*) Enter cost information from the consultants and the construction contractors, and record and track certifications for payment.

(*b*) Provide project cost tracking reports to the employer every month to indicate budgets, approved variations, pending variations, estimated cost to complete the project, certified payments, and variation from the original budget.

21.5 VARIATION ORDERS

(*a*) Develop and implement a system for review processing and tracking variation orders to ensure that all variation orders are accurately prepared and equitably negotiated by the consultants and project manager.

(*b*) Assist the consultants in developing cost estimates to validate contractors' variation proposals for completeness and accuracy.

22.0 COMMISSIONING AND HANDOVER PROGRAMME

(*a*) Identify all equipment and systems to be commissioned.

(*b*) Reference the programme for projected completion dates of the major building areas; and program testing, commissioning and handover activities accordingly.

(*c*) In conjunction with the architect, consultant, and contractor, determine completion and provide written notice to the employer that the work is ready for their final inspection and handover. Advise the employer in securing required guarantees, affidavits, releases, bonds and waivers and notify the contractor to turn over to employer all keys, manuals, record drawings and maintenance stocks.

Interact with the contractor and the employer to complete the commissioning and handover in accordance with the submitted program.

22.1 FF & E INSTALLATION

(*a*) The procured plant and equipment within the cost and quality parameters prescribed shall be installed when the building or services work is ready in the plant room. The installation is indicated in the FF & E Differentiation Statement.

(*b*) Similarly, the millwork and furnishing work in the guest rooms, food outlets and other public areas, including banquet hall, meeting rooms, pre-function areas (for more details, refer to Chapter: 08 - Duties of FF&EManager and concerned staff), should be completed.

22.2 TESTING AND COMMISSIONING

Testing and commissioning of electrical installations both on HT and LT sides. Testing and Commissioning mechanical work, chillers, chiller pump, firefighting equipment, generators and boiler will be carried out in a preplanned schedule and preferably by a separate team qualified to do the testing and commissioning. The completed work will be handed over to the Operator in the prescribed manner.

22.3 DISPOSAL OF DEBRIS

Disposal of construction debris is the individual contractor's responsibility leaving the area clean.

(Extra Useful Notes)

A.0 MISCELLANEOUS

A.1 GIVING NOTICE

Whenever any provision of contract documents requires the giving of written notice, it will be deemed to have been validly given if delivered in person to the individual or a member of the firm or an office of the company for whom it is intended, or if delivered at or sent by registered or certified mail, postage prepaid to the last business address known to the giver of the notice.

When any duration is referred to in the contract documents by days, it will be computed to exclude the first and include the last day of the said period. Suppose the last day of any such period falls on a Sunday or an official holiday by the law of the applicable jurisdiction, such day will be omitted from the computation.

A.2 NOTICE OF CLAIM

Should owner/employer or contractor suffer injury or damage to person or property because of any error, omission or act of the other party or any of the other party's employees or agents or others for whose actions the other party is legally liable, a claim will be made in writing to the other party within a reasonable time of the first observance of such injury or damage.

A.3 PROFESSIONAL FEES AND COURT COSTS INCLUDED

Whenever reference is made to claims, costs, losses and damages, it shall include in each case, but not be limited to all fees and charges of the project manager.

B.0 SUGGESTED PROJECT MANAGER'S STATUS DURING CONSTRUCTION

(To be incorporated in General Conditions of Contract)

B.1 OWNER/EMPLOYERS' REPRESENTATIVE

The project manager will be the owner/employer's representative during the construction period. The duties and responsibilities and the limitations of the project manager's authority as owner/employer's representative during construction are outlined in the contract documents. They shall not be extended without the owner/employer and project manager's written consent.

B.2 VISITS TO SITE

Project manager and owner/employer's consultant will make visits to the site at appropriate intervals during various stages of construction as project manager and owner/employer's consultant deems necessary, to observe as an experienced and qualified design professional the progress that has been made and the quality of the various aspects of the contractor's executed work. Based on information obtained during such visits and observations, the project manager and owner/employer consultants will endeavor for the benefit of the owner/employer to determine, in general, if the work is proceeding as per the contract documents. The project manager and owner/employer's consultant will not be required to make exhaustive or continuous on-site inspections to check the quality or quantity of the work. Project manager and owner/employer's consultant's efforts will be directed toward providing the owner/employer a greater degree of confidence that the completed work will generally conform to the contract documents. Based on such visits and on-site observations, the project manager will keep the owner/employer informed of the progress of the work and will endeavor to guard the latter against defective work. Owner/employer's consultant's visits and on-site observations are subject to all the limitations on project manager's and owner/employer's consultants authority and responsibility, but without limitation, during or as a result of owner/employer's consultant's on-site visits or observation of contractor's work project manager and owner/employer's consultant will not supervise, direct, control or have authority over or be responsible for contractor's means, methods, techniques, sequences or procedures of construction, or the safety precautions and programs incident to it, or for any failure of contractor to comply with laws and regulations applicable to the furnishing or performance of the work.

B.3 PROJECT REPRESENTATIVE

The project manager or his nominee will act as resident project representative for this contract for more continuous observation of the work. Responsibilities and authority and limitations thereof of such resident project representative and assistants will be applicable.

B.4 CLARIFICATIONS AND INTERPRETATIONS

Owner/employer's consultants will issue with reasonable promptness such written clarifications or interpretation of the requirements of the contract documents (in the form of drawings or otherwise) as project manager may determine necessary, which shall be consistent with the intent of any reasonably inferable from contract documents. Such written clarifications and interpretations will be binding on the contractor.

B.5 AUTHORISED VARIATIONS IN WORK

Owner/employer's consultant may recommend minor variations in the work from the requirements of the contract documents, which do not involve an adjustment in the contract price or the contract times and are compatible with the design concept of the completed project as a functioning whole as indicated by the contract documents. A field order may accomplish these and binding on the owner/employer, and the contractor, who shall perform the work involved promptly.

B.6 REJECTING DEFECTIVE WORK

The project manager will have authority to disapprove or reject work that is defective or does not produce a completed project conforming to the contract document or prejudice the integrity of the design concept of the completed project as a functioning whole as indicated by the contract documents. The project manager will also have the authority to inspect or test if work is fabricated, installed or completed.

B.7 DETERMINATIONS OF UNIT PRICES

The project manager will determine the actual quantities and classifications of unit price work performed by the contractor. They will review with contractor, the owner/employer's consultant preliminary determinations on such matters before rendering a written decision by recommendations of an application for payment or otherwise. The project manager's written decision thereon will be final and binding.

Owner/employer and contractor, unless, within ten days after the date of any such decision, either owner/employer or contractor delivers to the other and to project manager written notice of intention to appeal the project manager's decision and (*i*) an appeal from project manager's decision is taken within the time limits and in accordance with the procedures outlined in "dispute resolution agreement" entered into between owner/employer and contractor (*ii*) if no such dispute resolution agreement has been entered into, a formal proceeding is instituted by the appealing party in a forum of competent jurisdiction to exercise such rights or remedies as the appealing party may have,concerning project manager's decision unless otherwise agreed in writing by owner/employer and contractor.

B.8 LIMITATIONS ON PROJECT MANAGER'S AUTHORITY AND RESPONSIBILITIES

Neither project manager's authority or responsibility under other provision of the contract documents nor any decision made by project manager in good faith to exercise or not to exercise such authority or responsibility or the undertaking, exercise or performance of any authority or responsibility by project manager shall create, impose or give rise to any duty to contractor or any subcontractor or any supplier, and other person or organization, or to any surety for or employee or agent of any of them.

Project manager and owner/employer's consultant will not supervise, direct, control or have authority over or be responsible for contractor's means, methods, techniques, sequences or procedures of construction, or the safety precautions and programs incident thereto, or for any failure of the contractor to comply with laws and regulations applicable to the furnishing or performance of work. The project manager will not be responsible for the contractor's failure to perform or furnish the work in accordance with the contract documents.

Project manager will not be responsible for the acts or omissions of contractor or any subcontractor, any supplier, or any other person or organization performing or furnishing any of the work.

Project manager's review of the final application for payment and accompanying documentation and all maintenance and operating instructions, schedules, guarantees, bonds and certificates of inspection, tests and approvals and other documents required to be delivered will only be to determine generally that the content complies with the requirements of and in the case of certificate of inspections, test and approvals that the results certified indicate compliance with the contract documents.

B.9 CHANGE OF CONTRACT PRICE

The contract price constitutes the total compensation (subject to authorized adjustments) payable to the contractor for performing the work. All duties, responsibilities and obligations assigned to or undertaken by contractor shall be at contractor's expense without changing the contract price.

The value of any work covered by a change order or of any claim of an adjustment in the contract price will be determined as follows:

Where the work involved is covered by unit price contained in contract documents, by application such unit price.

Where the work involved is analogous to unit prices contained in the contract documents; the same shall be derived thereon.

Where the work is not covered by unit prices contained in the contract documents, not analogous to it, then the unit prices shall be arrived at based on the cost of material and labor plus 15% to cover the contractor's overheads and profit. However, if the work is done by a sub-contractor (nominated), the contractor's fee shall be restricted to 5%.

B.10 CHANGE OF CONTRACT TIMES

The contract times (or milestones) may only be changed by a change order or written amendment. Any claim for an adjustment of the contract times (or milestones) shall be based on written notice delivered by the project manager promptly (but in no event later than thirty days) after the occurrence of the event giving rise to the claim and stating the general nature of the claim. Notice of the extent of the claim with supporting data shall be delivered within sixty days after such occurrence (unless the project manager allows an additional period of time to ascertain more accurate data in support of the claim) and shall be accompanied by the claimant's written statement that the adjustment claimed is the total adjustment to which the claimant has reason to believe it entitled as a result of the occurrence of said event. The project manager shall determine all claims of adjustment in the contract times (or milestones).

C.0 SETTLEMENT OF DISPUTES

C.1 MATTERS TO BE SETTLED BY EMPLOYER

All disputes and differences of any kind whatsoever arising out of or in connection with the contract, whether during the progress of the works or after their completion, shall be referred by the contractor to the owner/employer, and they shall within a reasonable time after their presentation make and notify decisions thereon in writing.

The decisions, directions, clarifications, measurements, drawings and certificates with respect to any matter the decision for which is specially provided for by these or other special conditions to be given and made by the owner/employer or by the project manager and owner's consultants on behalf of the owner/employer are matters which are referred to from now on as excepted matters and shall be final and binding upon the contractor and shall not beset aside on account of non-observance of any formality, any omission, delay or error in proceeding or about the same or on any other grounds or for any reason and shall be without appeal.

In the event of any dispute or difference between the parties hereto as to the construction or operation of this contract, or the respective rights and liabilities of the parties on any matter in question, dispute or difference on the certificate to which the contractor may claim to be entitled, or if the owner/employer fails to make a decision within a reasonable time, then and in any such case, but except in any of the accepted matters referred to elsewhere in these general conditions, the contractor after 90 days of his presenting his final claim on the disputed matters, may demand in writing that the dispute or difference be referred to arbitration. Such in question, dispute or difference, and only such dispute or difference other than accepted matters of which the demand has been made, and no other dispute or difference shall be referred to the arbitration of an officer of the owner/employer to be nominated by the managing director at the relevant time by the board of directors of the owner/employer and as per the provision of the latest Indian Arbitration Act, in force at the time, shall apply to such arbitration.

C.2 ARBITRATION

The contractor shall not except with the consent in writing of the owner/employer or the owner's consultants, in any way delay the carrying out of the work by reason of any such matter, question or dispute being referred to arbitration but shall proceed with the work with all due diligence and shall, until the decision of the arbitration is given, abide by the decision of the project manager/owner's consultants and no award of the arbitrator shall relieve the contractor of his obligation to adhere strictly to the project manager/owner's consultants instructions with regard to the actual carrying out of the work except as specifically affected by such award.

8 CHAPTER

Duties of FF&E (Furniture Fittings & Equipment) Manager and Concerned Staff

Manager and the Concerned Staff

The operator's representative will also be associated when the FF&E work is planned and executed. In fact, a good operator will insist on even decision-making powers subject to budget, time and quality, mutually agreed upon with the owner. The FF&E differentiation table is prepared in advance with the concurrence of the architect, the interior designer and other consultants to avoid disruptions once the work starts.

FF&E differentiation table shown below is only an example. There could be variations in content depending on the volume and type of work.

Description	Budget	Design	Doc	Purchase	Install
Guest rooms/Suites/Guest Baths					
Furniture					
Bedding/bed frames	FOH/FF&E	I/OP	I	PUR	FI
Case goods (Movable)	FOH/FF&E	I	I	PUR	FI
Case goods (Fixed)	FOH/FF&E	I/A	I/A	MC	MC
Seating/Upholstery (Movable)	FOH/FF&E	I	I	PUR	FI
Seating/upholstery (Fixed)	FOH/FF&E	I	I	PUR	MC
Lamps/Lighting (Portable)	FOH/FF&E	I	I	PUR	Fi
Decorative Lighting (Fixed)	FOH/FF&E	I	I	PUR	GC
Bed Coverings	FOH/FF&E	I	I	PUR	FI/OP
Draperies/Window Covering	FOH/FF&E	I	I	PUR	FI
Decorative Mirrors (Loose)	FOH/FF&E	I	I	PUR	FI
Planters (Loose, Decorative)	FOH/FF&E	I	I	PUR	FI
Art work	ART	I	I	PUR	Fi
Floors					
Carpet Installation	C	I	I/V	C/PUR	GC
Carpet	FOH/FF&E	I	I	PUR	GC
Pad	FOH/FF&E	I	I	PUR	GC
Area Rugs	FOH/FF&E	I	I	PUR	FI

Marble/Granite/Stone/Tile Floor	C	I/A	A/I	GC	GC
Marble/Granite/stone/Tile Base	C	I/A	A/I	GC	GC
Wood Floor	C	I/A	A/I	GC	GC
Wood Base	C	I	I/A	MC	MC
Vinyl/Rubber Base	C	I	I/A	GC	GC
Ceilings					
Plaster/Gypsum Board (Painted)	C	I	A	GC	GC
Spray Texture on Slab	C	I/A	A	GC	GC
Acoustical	C	I/A	A	GC	GC
Special Ceilings, Metal	C	I	A/I	MC	MC
Special Ceilings, Fabric	FOH/FF&E	I	I/A	PUR	FI
Special Finishes, faux finish, gilding & Leafing	C	I	I	GC	GC
Crows Moulding/Cornice, Wood	C	I	I/A	GC	GC
Crown Moulding/Cornice,					
Plaster, GFRC	C	I	I/A	GC	GC
Wall Finishes					
Vinyl Wall covering	FOH/FF&E	I	I	PUR	GC
Paper wall covering	FOH/FF&E	I	I	PUR	GC
Paint/Duraplex	C	I	I/A	GC	GC
Fabric (direct apply)	FOH/FF&E	I	I	PUR	GC
Fabric (upholstered wall)	FOH/FF&E	I	I	PUR	FI/V
Marble/Granite/Stone/Tile	C	I	A	GC	GC
Wood Paneling	C	I	A	GC	GC
Doors					
Door Design, Entry, Closet, Bath, Connecting	C	I/A	A/I	GC	GC
Finishes	C	I	I/A	GC	GC
Hardware, decorative – door furniture	C	A/I	A	GC	GC
Hardware, hinges, closers, locks, silences, seals, etc.	C	A/I	A	GC	GC
Locking Systems	C	OP/I/A	A	GC	GC
Mill work	C	I/A	I/A	MC/GC	MC/GC
Louvered Doors/Shutters	C	I/A	I/A	MC/GC	MC/GC
Door Trim, Decorative	C	I/A	I/A	MC/GC	Mc/gc
Door Frames	C	A	A	GC	GC

Windows					
Window Design	C	A/I	A/I	GC	GC
Finishes	C	A	A/I	GC	GC
Hardware, decorative	C	I	A	GC	GC
Hardware,Hinges, Closers, Locks, Seats, etc.	C	A/I	A	GC	GC
Locking Systems	C	OP/I/A	A	GC	GC
Millwork	C	I/A	I/A	MC/GC	MC/GC
Shutters	C	I/A	I/A	MC/GC	MC/GC
Trim, Decorative	C	I/A	I/A	MC/GC	MC/GC
Window Frames	C	A	A	GC	GC
Window Coverings					
Draperies/Valance/Cornice – Fabrication, Rods, Tracks & Hardware	FOH/FF&E	I	I	PUR	FI
Blocking for Drapery/Valance/ Cornice	C	A/I	I	GC	GC
Shades/Blinds	FOH/FF&E	I	A/I	PUR	GC
Motorized Systems for Drapery/Blinds & Shades	FOH/FF&E	I/A/EE	A/EE	PUR	GC/V
Connection & Wiring for Motorized Systems	C	A/EE	EE	GC	GC
Connection & Wiring for above	C	A/EE	EE	GC	GC
Sun Screens/Shutters	C	I/A	A	GC	GC
Mill Work/Carpentry					
Standing & Running Trim	C	I/A	A/I	GC/MC	GC/MC
Closet Shelf and Rod	C	I/A	A/I	GC	GC
Vanity Millwork	C	I/A	A/I	GC/MC	GC/MC
Vanity Top	C	I/A	A/I	GC	GC
Blocking for Millwork	C	A	A	GC	GC
Blocking for Artwork/Framed Mirrors, case Goods	C	A/I	A	GC	GC
Other Blocking	C	A	A	GC	GC
Lighting					
Plug-In	FOH/FF&E	I	I	PUR	FI
Plug-In Light Bulbs	OS&E	OP/I	OP	OP	OP
Wall Sconce, Picture Lights	FOH/FF&E	I/LD	I	PUR	GC
J Box, Clock outlets Wall Sconce Installation	C	I/EE	EE	GC	GC
Architectural Fixtures					
Incandescent/Fluorescent/low voltage (Surface or Recessed)	C	I/A/LD	LD/A/ EE	GC	GC

Emergency Lighting	C	I/A/EE	EE/A	GC	GC
Switching/dimming	C	I/LD/A	LD/EE	GC	GC
Electrical					
Outlets/Complete System	C	I/OP/EE	EE	GC	GC
Cover Plates	C	I/A/EE	EE/A	GC	GC
Mechanical/Plumbing					
Fan Coil Unit/HVAC Systems	C	ME/A/OP	ME	GC	GC
Decorative Grills	C	I/A/ME	A/ME	GC	GC
Thermostat (locations)	C	I/A/ME	ME	GC	GC
Exhaust Systems	C	ME/A	ME	GC	GC
Plumbing/Piping/Connections Valving, etc.	C	PE	PE	GC	GC
Plumbing fixtures, sanitary ware, fixtures, faucets, bath accessories	C	I/OP/A	PE	GC	GC
Life Safety					
Sprinkler System	C	A/FP	FP	GC	GC
Smoke Detector	C	EE/A/FP	EE	GC	GC
Audio and Visual Annunciation/ Communication Systems	C	A/EE/FP	EE	GC	GC
Fire hose/Extinguisher/Pull stations/Alarms	C	A/EE/FP	EE/A/I	GC	GC
Signage	OS&E	GD	GD	PUR	FI/OP
Telephone					
Conduit, Pull wire, Sleeves, Boxes	C	OP/EE/V	EE	GC	GC
Cover Plates	C	I/A/EE	A/EE	GC	GC
Telephone, Desk, Bedside, Bath	OS&E	OP/S/I	OP/S/A	Op	V/OP
Television/Anetna					
Conduit, Pull Wire Sleeves, boxes, Cable	C	OP/I/EE/V	EE	GC	GC
Cable/Cover Plate	C	OP/I	OP/A/ EE	GC	GC
Television Set	OS&E	Op	Op	OP	V
Movie System	OS&E	Op	Op	Op	V
VCR/VCP/CD	OS&E	OP	Op	OP	V
Misc. Guestrooms					
Bed Lines, Pillows & Blankets	OS&E	I/OP	I/OP	PUR	Op
Radio, Clock, Clock Radio	OS&E	OP	OP	PUR	FI/OP
Mini Bar, Refrigerator	OS&E	I/OP	I/OP	PUR	FI
Safe	OS&E	I/OP	I/OP	PUR	FI
Tie Rack/Shoe Rack	OS&E	I/OP	I/OP	PUR	FI/MC

Robe Hooks	OS&E	I/OP	I/OP	PUR	FI/OP
Fixed Mirrors	C	I/A	I/A	GC	GC
Misc. Guest Bath					
Bath Accessories	C	OP/I/A	I/A	GC	GC
Shower Rod	C	OP/I/AI	I/A	GC	GC
Shower Curtain	FOH/FF&E	I	I	PUR	FI
Liner	OS&E	OP/I	I/OP	PUR	FI
Shower Door	C	I/A	I/A	GC	GC
Clothesline	C	OP	I/A	GC	GC
Fixed Mirror	C	I	I/A	GC	GC
Bath Magnified Shaving Mirror, Lighted	C	OP/I	I/OP/EE	PUR	GC
Shaving Mirror, Unlighted	C	OP/I	I/OP	PUR	GC
Public Areas/Guest Corridor/ Passenger Lift Lobbies					
Furniture					
Case Goods (movable)	FOH/FF&E	I	I	PUR	FI
Case goods (fixed)	FOH/FF&E	I/A	I/A	MC	MC
Seating/Upholstery (movable)	FOH/FF&E	I	I	PUR	FI
Seating/Upholstery (fixed)	FOH/FF&F	I	I	PUR*	MC*
Lamps/Lighting (Portable)	FOH/FF&E	I	I	PUR	FI
Decorative Lighting (fixed)	FOH/FF&E	I	I/LD/EE	PUR	GC
Chandeliers – dressing (hanging crystals)	FOH/FF&E	I	I/LD/EE	PUR	FI/V
Draperies/Window Covering	FOH/FF&E	I	I	PUR	FI
Decorative Mirrors (loose)	FOH/FF&E	I	I	PUR	FI
Mirrors (Fixed)	C	I	I/A	GC	GC
Planters (Loose)	FOH/FF&E	I/LS	I/LS	PUR	FI
Planters (fixed)	C	I/A/LS	I	GC	GC
Irrigation for Planters	C	LS/I	LS	GC	GC
Ash Urns (decorative)	FOH/FF&E	I	I	PUR	FI
Art work	ART	I	I	PUR	FI
Blocking for artwork mirrors, case goods	C	I/A	A	GC	GC
Floors					
Carpet Installation	C	I	I/V	C/PUR	GC
Carpet	FOH/FF&E	I	I	PUR	GC
Pad	FOH/FF&E	I	I	PUR	GC
Area Rugs	FOH/FF&E	I	I	PUR	FI
Marble/Granite/Stone/Tile Floor	C	I/A	A/I	GC	GC

Marble/Granite/Stone/Tile Base	C	I/A	A/I	GC	GC
Wood Floor	C	I/A	A/I	GC	GC
Wood Base	C	I	I/A	MC	MC
Vinyl/Rubber Base	C	I	I/A	GC	GC
Thresholds, Saddles, Transition Strips	C	I/A	I/A	GC	GC
Ceilings					
Plaster/Gypsum Board	C	I	A	GC	GC
Acoustical	C	I/A	A	GC	GC
Articulated Gyp, Soffits, Coffers (Painted)	C	I	A	GC	GC
Special Ceilings, wood	C	I	A/I	MC	MC
Special Ceilings, metal	C	I	A/I	MC	MC
Special Ceilings, fabric	FOH/FF&E	I	I/A	PUR	FI
Crown Moulding/Cornice, Wood	C	I	I/A	GC	GC
Crown Moulding/Cornice, Plaster, GFRC	C	I	I/A	GC	GC
Special finishes, Faux Finishes, Gilding & Leading	C	I	I	GC	GC
Murals/Frescoes	FOH/FF&E	I/V	I/V	PUR	V
Wall Finishes					
Vinyl Wall Covering	FOH/FF&E	I	I	PUR	GC
Paper Wall covering	FOH/FF&E	I	I	PUR	GC
Paint/Dura flex	C	I	I/A	GC	GC
Fabric (Direct apply)	FOH/FF&E	I	I	PUR	GC
Fabric (Upholstered wall)	FOH/FF&E	I	I	PUR	FI/V
Corner Guards	C	I	I/A	GC	GC
Marble/Granite/Stone/Tile	C	I	A/I	GC	GC
Wood Paneling	C	I	I/A	MC	MC
Special Finishes, Faux finishes, gilding and Leafing	C	I/V	I/V	PUR/GC	V
Murals/Frescoes	FOH/FF&E	I/V	I/V	PUR	V
Doors					
Door Design	C	I/A	A/I	GC	GC
Finishes	C	I	I/A	GC	GC
Hardware, decorative – door furniture	C	A/I	A	GC	GC
Hardware, hinges, closers, locks, silencers, seals, panic bars/hardware	C	A/I	A	GC	GC

Locking Systems	C	OP/I/A	A	GC	GC
Hardware	C	I/A	A	GC	GC
Millwork	C	I/A	I/A	GC/MC	GC/MC
Door Trim, Decorative	C	I/A	I/A	GC/MC	GC/MC
Door Frames	C	I/A	A	GC	GC
Storefronts (Metal)	C	A/I	A/I	GC	GC
Storefronts (Wood)	C	I/A	I/A	MC/GC	MC/GC
Movable Partitions	C	I/A	A/SE/I	GC	GC
Partition Finish	C	I	I/A	GC	MC/GC
Windows					
Window Design	C	A/I	A	GC	GC
Finishes	C	I	A/I	GC	GC
Hardware, decorative	C	I	A	GC	GC
Hardware, hinges, closers, locks, seats, etc.	C	A/I	A	GC	GC
Locking Systems	C	OP/I/A	A	GC	GC
Millwork	C	I/A	I/A	MC/GC	MC/GC
Shutters	C	I/A	I/A	MC/GC	MC/GC
Trim, Decorative	C	I/A	I/A	MC/GC	MC/GC
Window Frames	C	A	A	GC	GC
Retail Storefronts					
Storefronts (Metal)	C	A/I	A/I	GC	GC
Storefronts (Wood)	C	I/A	I/A	MC/GC	MC/GC
Windows Coverings					
Draperies/Valance/Cornice – Fabrication, Rods, Tracks & Hardware	FOH/FF&E	I	I	GC	FI
Blocking for Drapery track, Valance/Cornice	C	A/I	A	GC	GC
Shades/Blinds, (Decorative)	FOH/FF&E	I	I	PUR	FI
Motorized Systems for Drapery/Blinds & shades	FOH/FF&E	I/A/EE	A/EE	FF&E	GC/V
Connection & Wiring for above	C	A/EE	EE	GC	GC
Sun Screens/Shading (Interior)	FOH/FF&E	I/A	A/I	PUR	FI
Sun Screens/Shading (Exterior)	C	A/I	A	GC	GC
Shutters	C	I/A	I/A	MC/GC	MC/GC
Mill Work					
Wood Paneling including matching standing & running trim.	C	I	I/A	MC/GC	MC/GC

Cabinetry (Front Desk, Concierge, Bellman, Valet)	C	I	I	MC/GC	MC/GC
Equipment	OS&E/BOH	OP/I	OP	OP	OP
Bars/Service Stations/Buffers	C	I	I/KC	MC/GC	MC/GC
Bars/Service Stations/Buffet Equipment	OS&E/BOH	KC/OP/I	KC	GC/KC	GC
Cabinets & Counters	C	I	I/A	MC/GC	MC/GC
Marble/Granite/Stone Tops and Surrounds	C	I	I/A	MC/GC	MC/GC
Screens/wood storefront	C	I/A	I/A	MC/GC	MC/GC
Vanity Tops/Apron/Surround	C	I/A	I/A	MC/GC	MC/GC
Telephone Counters	C	I/A	I/A	GC	MC/GC
Booth/banquettes	C	I	I/A	GC	MC/GC
In-wall Blocking	C	A/V	A/V	GC	GC
Lighting					
Plug-In	FOH/FF&E	I	I	PUR	FI
Light bulbs for Plug-In	OS&E	I/V	I/V	OP	OP
Wall Sconce	FOH/FF&E	I	I	PUR	GC
Picture Lights	FOH/FF&E	I	I	PUR	FI*
J Box, Clock Outlets	C	I/EE	EE	GC	GC
Wall Sconce Installation	C	I/EE	I/EE	GC	GC
Chandeliers (Including assembly & dressing with crystals)	FOH/FF&E	I/LD	I/LD/EE	PUR	GC
Chandelier light bulbs	OS&E	I/V	I/V	PUR	GC/OP
Lighting @ Millwork	C	I/LD	I/LD/A	GC	GC
Support for chandeliers	C	V/SE	SE	GC	GC
Architectural Lighting (Down lights, Cove lights, strip lighting, Track lighting, etc. Incandescent/Fluorescent/Low Voltage)	C	LD/1	LD/EE	GC	GC
Light Bulbs for Architectural Lighting	C	LD/I/A/EE	LD/EE	GC	GC
Emergency Lighting	C	LD/IA/EE	EE/A	GC	GC
Switching & Dimming	C	LD/I	LD/EE	GC	GC
Graphics/Signage					
Interior Signage	C	GD/OP/I	GD	PUR	FI/V
Exterior Signage	C	GD/OP	GD	PUR/GC	GC/V
Specialty Signage (Room Identity)	C	GD/OP	GD	PUR	FI/V
Menus/Guest-room compendiums/guest Amenities	OS&E	GD/OP	GD	OP	OP

Events Monitors	OS&E	I/GD	GD	FF&E	FI/GC
Plants/Planters					
Fixed Planters	C	I/A/LS	I	MC/GC	MC/GC
Movable Planters	FOH/FF&E	I/LS	I	PUR	FI
Plant Material (Interior)	OS&E	I/LS	I/LS	OP	OP/V
Plant Material (Exterior)	C	LS	LS	GC	LS/GC/V
Irrigation	C	LS	LS/A	GC	GC
System Equipment					
Electrical					
Outlets/Complete System (including location)	C	I/EE	EE	GC	GC
Cover Plates	C	I/A/EE	EE/A	GC	GC
Mechanical/Plumbing					
Water Features (Including Speciality Pools)	C	WF/LS	WF/LS	GC	GC
HVAC Systems	C	ME/A/OP	ME	GC	GC
Decorative Grill	C	I/A/ME	A/ME	GC	GC
Thermostat (Location)	C	I/A/ME	A/ME	GC	GC
Exhaust Systems	C	ME/A	ME	GC	GC
Plumbing/Piping/Connections, etc.	C	PE	PE	CG	CG
Plumbing Fixtures, Sanitary Ware, Fixtures, Faucets, Accessories	C	I/OP/A	PE	GC	GC
Drinking Fountains	C	I/A	A/PE	GC	GC
Life Safety					
Sprinkler System (Location)	C	A/I/FP	FP	GC	GC
Smoke Detector	C	EE/A/FP	EE/A	GC	GC
Fire Alarm & Enunciator	C	EE/A/FP	EE/A	GC	GC
Audio & Visual Annunciation/ Communication Systems	C	EE/A/FP	EE/A	GC	GC
Audio & Visual Alarm/Strobes/ Lights	C	EE/A/FP	EE/A	GC	GC
Fire Cabinet and Hose	C	FP/A/I	FP/A	GC	GC
Fire Extinguisher	C	FP/A/I	A	GC	GC
Signage	C/OS&E	GD	GD	PUR	FI/OP
Telephone					
Conduit, Pull wire, Sleeves, Boxes	C	OP/EE/V	EE	GC	GC
Cover Plates	C	I/A/EE	EE	GC	GC
Equipment	OS&E	OP/S	OP/S	OP	V

Audio/Visual Equipment/Sound System/PA					
Conduit, Pull wire, Sleeves, Boxes	C	I/EE	EE	GC	GC
Equipment	BOH	OP/AV	Op	Op	V
Lecterns	OS&E	I/OP/AV	OP/AV	Op	OP
Projection Screens (Built-In)	OS&E	I/OP/AV	I/A/AV	OP	GC
Speakers	C	I/AV/SC	A/SC/EE	GC	GC
Blackboards, White Boards, Tack Surfaces (Fixed)	BOH	I/OP	OP	PUR	MC/FI
Blackboards, White Boards, Tack Surfaces (Portable)	OS&E	OP	OP	PUR	OP
Television/Antenna					
Conduit, Pull Wire Sleeves, Boxes, Cable	C	OP/I/EE/V	EE	GC	GC
Cable/Cover Plate	C	OP/I	OP/A/EE	GC	V
Television Set	OS&E	OP	OP	OP	V
Movie System	OS&E	OP	OP	OP	V
VCR/VCP/CD/Stereo	OS&E	Op	Op	OP	V
Kitchen/Bar Equipment					
General Kitchen Equipment	C	KC	KC	CG	GC
Bar/Service Station Equipment	C	KC	KC	GC	GC
Show Kitchen Equipment	C	KC	KC	GC	GC/V
Rough-In/Installation	C	KC/ME/EE	KC/ME/EE	GC	GC
Ice and Vending					
Ice Machine	BOH	KC	KC	PUR	FI
Ice Machine Drain/					
Rough-In/Connect Equipment	C	KC/MEEE	KC/ME/EE	GC	GC
Back-of-House/Service Areas					
FURNITURE (Breakdown Buffets, etc.)					
Case goods (movable)	BOH	I/Op	I/OP	PUR	FI
Case goods (fixed)	BOH	A/OP	A/OP	MC	MC
Banquet Tables	BOH	OP	OP	PUR	FI/OP
Seating/Upholstery (movable)	BOH	OP	OP	PUR	FI
Seating/Upholstery(fixed)	BOH	A/OP	A/OP	PUR	MC
Banquet Chairs	BOH	I/OP	I	PUR	FI
Lamps/Lighting (Portable)	BOH	OP	OP	PUR	FI
Decorative Lighting (Fixed)	BOH	OP	OP	PUR	GC
Draperies/Window Covering	BOH	OP	OP	PUR	FI

Decorative Mirrors (Loose)	BOH	OP	OP	PUR	FI
Planters (Loose, decorative)	BOH	OP	OP	PUR	FI
Artwork	BOH	OP	OP	PUR	FI
Shelving (Movable)	BOH/OS&E	OP	OP	PUR	FI
Shelving (Fixed)	C	A/OP	A	GC	GC
Files/Storage	BOH	A/OP	OP	PUR	FI
Floors					
Sealed Concrete	C	A	A	GC	CG
Resilient	C	A	A	GC	GC
Carpet Installation	C	?	V	PUR/GC	GC
Carpet Pad	BOH	OP	I	PUR/GC	GC
Carpet	BOH	A	A	PUR	GC
Wood Flooring	C	A	A	GC	GC
Marble/Granite/Stone/Slate Tile Flooring	C	A/I	A	GC	GC
Wood Base	C	A	A	GC	GC
Marble/Granite/Stone/Slate/ Tile Base	C	A	A	GC	GC
Stage/Dance Floor (Portable)	OS&E	OP	OP	OP	OP
Thresholds/Reducer Strips/ Transition Strips	C	A	A	GC	GC
Metal Transition Strips	C	A	A	GC	GC
Ceilings					
Dry Wall	C	A	A	GC	GC
Acoustical Ceilings	C	A	A	GC	GC
Painted/Texture on Structures	C	A	A	GC	GC
Wall Finishes					
Paint	C	I/A	A	GC	GC
Vinyl Wall Covering	BOH/FF&E	A	A	PUR	GC
Marble/Granite/Stone/Tile	C	A	A	GC	GC
Corner Guards/Bumpers	C	A/OP	A	GC	GC
Toilet Partitions					
Metal/laminate	C	A	A	GC	GC
Movable Partitions					
Movable Partitions	C	A	A/SE	GC	GC
Partition Finish	C/BOH	A	A	PUR/GC	MC/GC
Doors					
Design	C	A	A	GC	GC
Finishers	C	A	I/A	GC	GC
Hardware, Decorative – Door Furniture	C	A	A	GC	GC

Hardware, Hinges, Closers, Locks, Silencers, Seals, Panic bars/Hardware	C	A	A	GC	GC
Locking Systems	C	OP/A	A	GC	GC
Hardware	C	A	A	GC	GC
Millwork	C	A	A	GC/MC	GC/MC
Door Trim, Decorative	C	A	A	GC/MC	GC/MC
Door Frames	C	A	A	GC	GC
Windows					
Window Design	C	A	A	GC	GC
Finishes	C	A	A	GC	GC
Hardware, decorative	C	A	A	GC	GC
Hardware, Hinges, closers, locks, seals, etc.	C	A	A	GC	GC
Locking Systems	C	OP/A	A	GC	GC
Millwork	C	A	I/A	MC/GC	MC/GC
Shutters	C	A	I/A	MC/GC	MC/GC
Trim, Decorative	C	A	I/A	MC/GC	MC/GC
Window Frames	C	A	A	GC	GC
Window Coverings					
Drapery/Valance/Cornice Fabrication, Rods & Hardware	BOH	OP	OP/I	PUR	FI
Blocking for Rod, Drapery/ Valance/Cornice	C	A	A	GC	GC
Shades/Blinds	BOH	OP	OP	PUR	FI
Window Shutters	C	A	A	GC	GC/MC
Sun Screens	C	A	A	GC	GC
Lighting					
Plug-In	BOH	OP	OP	PUR	FI
Plug-In Bulbs	OS&E	OP	OP	OP	OP
Wall Sconce/Picture Lights	BOH	LD	LD/EE	PUR	GC
Architectural fixed lighting (Down lights, cove, strip, track lighting)	C	LD/EE	EE/A/ LD	GC	GC
Light Bulbs	C	LD/EE	EE	GC	GC
Special Lighting	BOH	LD	EE/LD	PUR	FI
J Boxes/Block Outlets for FF&E Lighting	C	I/LD/EE	EE	GC	GC
Structural Support for Chandeliers	C	SE/A	SE/A	GC	GC
Stage/Exhibit Lighting	C	LD	LD/EE	GC	GC

Rigging/Pull-Down Devices for Accent Lighting	C	LD/EE	LD/EE	GC	GC
Lifts					
Passenger Lifts					
Cab Interior walls and Ceilings	C	I/A	I/A	GC	MC
Carpet Installation	C	I	I/V	C/PUR	GC
Carpet	FOH	I	I	PUR	GC
Pad	FOH	I	I	PUR	GC
Area Rugs	FOH	I	I	PUR	FI
Marble/Granite/Stone/Tile Floor	C	I/A	A/I	GC	GC
Marble/Granite/Stone/Time Base	C	I/A	A/I	GC	GC
Wood Floor	C	I/A	A/I	GC	GC
Wood Base	C	I	I/A	MC	MC
Door Exterior and Interior	C	I	I/A	GC	GC
Door Frame and Sill (Metal work)	C	A/I	A	GC	GC
Decorative Lighting	FOH/FF&E	I/LD	I/EE/LD	PUR	GC
Call Numbers/Buttons	C	I	I/A/EE/ GD	GC	GC
Hall Lanterns/Floor Indicators	C	I/A	I/A	GC	GC
Motor, Controls, etc.	C	A/EC	A/EE	GC	GC
Life Safety	C	A/EE/I	A/EE	GC	GC
Telephone	C	OP/EC	A/EE	GC	GC
Service Lifts					
Finishes (All Surfaces)	C	A	A	GC	GC
Lighting	C	A/EE	A/EE	GC	GC
Motor, Controls, etc.	C	A	A/EE	GC	GC
Call Numbers/Buttons	C	A/OP	A/EE	GC	GC
Hall Lanterns/Floor Indicators	C	A	A	GC	GC

Legend

A	Architect
ART	Artwork Designer
AV	Audio-Visual
C	Consultant
DOC	Documentation
EE	Electrical Engineer
FC	Fitness Centre

FI	Furnishing Installer
FOH	Front of the House
FP	Fire Prevention
GC	General Construction Contractor
GD	Graphic Designer
I	Interior Designer
KC	Kitchen Consultant
LD	Lighting Design
LS	Landscaping
MC	Millwork Contractor
ME	Mechanical Engineering
O	Operator
OP	Operations
OS&E	Operations, Supplies & Equipment
PE	Project Engineer
PUR	Purchase
SE	Structural Engineer
V	Vendor
WF	Water Features

CHAPTER 9
Risks with COVID-19 and Corrections

9.1 INTRODUCTION

The recent COVID 19 pandemic has left the world shaken in its aftermath and hospitality sector has been the worst hit. Many hotels and resorts have been shut down, and investors are worried about recovery, if and when. Several Covid vaccines have been discovered and administered, yet variants are bound to give the jitters. Irrespective of vaccination, certain fundamental changes in the hospitality field would be necessary if people in this business hope to survive. The economy will not thrive, let alone improve, when a vital limb of the economy stops working.

Therefore, one feels the following changes in the facilities are called for:

1. Guest rooms - In twin rooms, beds can be positioned to ensure at least two meters of distance between them. King rooms can only be single occupancy.
2. Each guest should be supplied with/carry a sanitizer spray. Apart from the hotel room sanitization before the guest occupies, individuals should follow sanitization protocols at all times. Bath tubs should be avoided in twin rooms.
3. Used linen should be put in paper bag by the guest, and this should be picked up by the maid and put in the washing machine directly, and trash bag segregated appropriately. Beds should have a layer of washable rubber sheets which should be changed for every guest and washed.
4. Jacuzzis must be avoided unless meant for individual use only.
5. The buffet cannot be displayed and kept exposed. All buffet items have to be in containers with lids, operated by the steward in attendance and served to the guest carrying the plate. The menu can be displayed electronically.
6. Dinner plates, spoons and forks have to be washed and sanitized before each use.
7. Dining tables, which used to be 4′ × 4′ in size, should be minimum of 5′ × 5′. The tables have to be sanitized for each guest.
8. Swimming pools should be avoided. There should be individual bathing cubicles with ground glass doors and sanitized before every use.
9. The bathing cubicles should be in open ground on a hard surface arranged in an "H" shape to allow ladies and other guests to use them separately and be sanitized between each use. The Sun-bathing chairs should be adjusted for social distancing and suitably placed on either side of the "H" shaped cubicles. Bathing towels

should be in paper bags and should to be put back in the paper bag after use and taken to the laundry.

10. The banqueting has to have tables with a maximum of two occupants.
11. Lobby lounge should follow social distancing.
12. Convention center should see that the participants' tables are separated adequately and at least two meters wide.
13. Sauna and steam baths have to be planned separately for individual use in the health club. Massage parlors may have to be discontinued.

CHAPTER 10

Scope for Hotels & Resorts in India

10.1 INTRODUCTION

As mentioned earlier, hotels and resorts along with travel and tourism constitute 25% of a developed economy. A country like India with no oil reserves and no money to speak of should utilize its demographic dividend in the service sector, using whatever natural resources it has. Moreover, India is trying to overcome past grievances as a subject nation. Even after attaining freedom, fifty years went by without significant progress and much less in the hospitality sector. Accepting a truncated India by the founding fathers left the country war-ravaged with a bleak economy.

Of course, there were a few silver linings. Scientists Dr. Homi J. Bhabha, Dr. Vikram Sarabhai and their teams ushered in a "Nuclear India" and made India a "Space Power". Dr. Swaminathan, the agricultural scientist, steered in the "Green Revolution" and helped India overcome hunger. Dr. Joseph Kurien led "Operation Flood". Mr. Narayana Murthy and his associates heralded the "Information Technology" boom, which empowered millions of Indian engineers with jobs and ultimately made India another "Silicon Valley". Mr. E. Sreedharan made Konkan Railway a reality, strengthened public transport with metro rail, and thus gained the moniker, "Metro Man". Prime Minister P V Narasimha Rao opened the economy in 1991 to market forces, followed by Prime Minister Atal Bihari Vajpayee who started commissioning much-needed infrastructure such as highways, waterways, railways, airports, ports and harbors. Under the current dispensation, there has been greater push and India now has around 1,30,000 kilometers of highways and 60 operating airports with 100 more on the anvil. In 2009, there were hardly 10,000 branded hotel rooms. Concerted action since then has had a leapfrog effect. Per its latest (2019) report, the tourism industry mentioned India's inland tourist strength to have gone up to US$ 2.8 billion and foreign tourists accounting to 2 million and the revenue from tourism including hotels and resorts as US$ 250 billion. However it is far too low compared to those countries considered economically backward than us. The report states that there are only 130,000 branded hotel rooms in India, while there should have been at least 500,000 branded rooms by now.

Unless foreign investment flows in to the hotel and hospitality sector, there will be no progress worth the name. Unless we create conditions to sell our goods or services and facilitate currency inflow, Indian economy may show little improvement.

For example, Bali, called "Paradise on Earth," is an island of only 5,600 sq. km in area, next to the island of Java in the Indonesian Archipelago. It has two airport terminals, one national and another an international airport at stone's throw from each other. Bali has no archaeological marvels as we do; there are no big industries, no steel plants, no big highways or underpasses or clover junctions. There are no cement plants, automobile industries, railways, ports or harbors, sky scrapers, or even concrete jungles. But the island does have several beaches, green countryside, and cultivated fields along its coast. It is like any typical Indian village, but the similarity ends there. The surroundings are fabulous, neat and clean, and the houses - miniature temples. One can see rice paddies and men farmers wearing dhoti tucked up in Tamil style with a towel wrapped around their head in Karnataka style and a shirt top, and the women wearing a sarong-like dress. The island is dotted with a few temples with tiered roofs, like the Uluwatu temple. Also, one can see Gaja Gruha (Ganesh Temple) and Shiva Temple surrounded by greenery and sprawling water bodies, landscaped gardens, some of them with exotic trees and low boundaries.

The shopping areas in the villages are fully equipped with crafted wood and batik silks. The roads have small open-air stadia, with audience seated in covered galleries and dance themes mostly sequences from Indian epics. Every place is spotlessly clean, and there is no pollution. Resort development areas like Nusa Dua in Kuta, Samuh, Negara in Jembra and Seminyak have numerous hotels and resorts to suit every purse ranging from US$50 to US$1500 a day. You can pick and choose the one that you can afford. Every resort has a picturesque reception, open lounges with landscaped scenery, freshwater bodies spread around the hotels, guest rooms, restaurants and cottages, and VIP and VVIP suite blocks with connecting corridors. There are at least four to five specialty restaurants in many resorts, with spas, gymnasiums and beautiful swimming pools. There are open-air dance floors in the spaces between the shopping arcade and eateries where Balinese artistes perform scenes from Mahabharata and Ramayana with seating arrangements all around, for the guests.

The sea waters are azure blue, crystal clear and the beaches spotlessly clean (locals are strictly out of bounds). Nusa Dua and other resort areas have about 40 top-class resorts, and Kuta beach has many small hotels and restaurants of 3 & 4 star categories. Bali may have more than 20,000 branded rooms. For a small island of 5600 Sq. Kms and 42 lakh population, the GDP in 2019 was nearly USD 60 Billion, with per capita income of USD 4200.

While it is impossible to create a Bali in India, it is possible to develop in India "conditions" where sun and sand are aplenty with comfortable temperature-controlled holiday accommodation, tropical surroundings with greenery, freshwater, 24 × 7 food and beverage with specialty cuisine, latest communication facilities, meeting rooms for business, cultural shows in open or covered auditoriums, halls for conferences and banquet hall, laundry, spa, gymnasium and a beach with azure blue rolling seas and crystal sands, facilities for beach sports or water activities, facility to visit wildlife parks and places of archaeological interest etc. And with adequate security for life and property, without infringing privacy or undesirable interference from local labor unions, politicians, unauthorized organizations and drug peddlers. Also, with each cluster not more than an hour's flight from a national/ international airport. There is abundant sun and sand along the western and eastern coasts of peninsular India. The coastline extends over 11,000 Kms in Gujarat, Maharashtra, Goa (one), Karnataka, Kerala, Tamil Nadu, Andhra, Orissa and West Bengal. It would not be difficult to identify a 25 Kms shoreline for each cluster at 25 such locations in the nine states of India from Gujarat to West Bengal, free from cyclones and tsunamis, with relative elevation. The cluster could also be a part of the Smart City principle with some essential additions such as educational centers, auxiliary industries, etc.

Cost parameters worked out indicate 25 clusters of 50 resorts each in a cluster, with 25 5-star resorts and 25 3-star resorts, spread over 1600 acres for each cluster including infrastructure (Please see Annexure-09: Eco Resorts). Clusters eventually work out more economical as a sub-structural part of the infrastructure, which can be done on a B-O-T basis, saving investment for the investor and with no burden on the Government.

A Resort Development Authority (RDA) could be created at the Center with all associated ministries represented. This authority could be a "Single Window" for the investor - Indian or foreign. The nine states mentioned above can have regional offices located in the state capitals and its representatives at each cluster. The land for the resort has to be allotted to the prospective hotelier along with water and electricity. Facilities for staff colony, staff amenities, hospitals for both the guest and the staff, malls with multiplexes, greenhouses, ultra-modern sports stadia for football, hockey, cricket, basketball, volleyball and golf courses for each cluster have to be created. Air-conditioned buses for guests to travel to four or five local places of interest, two light aircraft like Fokker and Dornier for the guests' convenience to fly to and from the nearest airport can be provided with an 8-laned highway adjoining the cluster, wide enough for the landing of a light aircraft. These facilities like land shore improvement against wave action, tsunami, etc., could be charged to the hotelier on an actual cost basis and recoverable in 20 annual installments @ 5% simple interest not exceeding 10% of the investment. Thus, lay the red carpet for an investor.

The investment by the investor works out to about USD 94 billion except the land part of it plus maintenance, which will be another USD 9.4 billion. So the total investment comes to approximately USD 104 billion. The additional expenditure on balance infrastructure run on BOT (Build, Operate and Transfer) basis works at USD 23 billion not to be charged to the investor. The whole project in Phases I, II and III is expected to take about eight years for completion with eight plus one clusters completed in the 4th year, eight more in the 6th year and eight more in the 8th year. The project on completion, along with travel, is expected to yield revenue of USD 300 billion per year (please see Annexure-09).The employment potential for the construction is 5.5 lakhs during the project duration of about eight years. The permanent employment will be for nearly 700,000 persons, almost all qualified and skilled. We may have to add ten international airports depending on the final locations for the clusters. Goa, with one cluster, can have a convention hall of 'international' scale. If the chosen locations have a hilly background, it will be rather regal apart from giving form and shape to the structures.

With architects like I.M. Quadri, Raj Rewal, Rajendra Kumar, Jasbir Sawhney, and engineers like Dr. Jain, Abhay Ghate, STUP, Nagendra (Sterling), any big project can be accomplished quickly. Foreign investors will bring their expertise, adding to the grandeur of the project.

सर्वेभवन्तुसुखिनः सर्वे सन्तु निरामयाः।

सर्वे भद्राणि पश्यन्तु मा कश्चिद्दुःखभाग्भवेत्।।

(Let all become happy, healthy and free from diseases. Let everyone find better fortune in their life. Let no one face any sorrow because of difficulties.)

ANNEXURE-01: Techno-Economic Feasibility Report for a 5-Star Hotel must Contain the Following

1. A preface giving the background, method of approach.
2. An executive summary consisting of:
    (*a*) Description of the proposed project
    (*b*) Current accommodation available (rooms) in the city
    (*c*) Projected demand (rooms) as per tourism corporation estimate
    (*d*) Future supply and demand
    (*e*) Segment-wise demand
    (*f*) Average room occupancy expected
    (*g*) Seasonal and overall occupation
    (*h*) Total revenue projected
    (*i*) Revenue projected in 6th year
    (*j*) Gross operating profit in 6th year
3. Introduction:
    (*a*) Promoter
    (*b*) Collaboration, if any
    (*c*) Consultants
    (*d*) Market
    (*e*) Market survey and Financial feasibility study
    (*f*) Method of approach for the market survey.
4. General information of location:
    (*a*) General
    (*b*) Geography
    (*c*) Climate
    (*d*) Population
    (*e*) Communication
    (*f*) Air travel connectivity

(*g*) Tourist arrival
(*h*) Factors affecting development and of Hotels, if any such as:
  (*i*) Political uncertainty and stability
  (*ii*) Business and Industrial development
  (*iii*) Banquet Facilities and entertainment in Hotels

5. Hotels - Supply and demand (Unit wise occupancy project for 10 years)
6. The proposed project:
   (*a*) Site
   (*b*) Development plans & recommendations
   (*c*) Hotel rooms of different types
   (*d*) Restaurants & Bar
   (*e*) Function rooms
   (*f*) Club & other facilities
   (*h*) Envisages demand
   (*i*) Seasonal occupation
   (*j*) Market composition
   (*k*) Calculation of overall food rate
   (*l*) Published tariffs
7. Preliminary architectural planning:
   (*a*) Salient features
   (*b*) Statement of F.A.R area
   (*c*) Built-up area statement
   (*d*) Summary of built-up area
   (*e*) Pre-design estimated cost
   (*f*) Implementation schedule
8. Financial Projections:
   (*a*) Room revenue
   (*b*) Food revenue
   (*c*) Banquet food revenue
   (*d*) Cost of sales
   (*e*) Payable expenditure
   (*f*) Transfer to replacement reserves
   (*g*) Management fees (% of Room Revenue & % of Gross Profit before tax)
   (*h*) Project cost
   (*i*) Means of finance
   (*j*) Depreciation
   (*k*) Taxation
9. Consultants' organizational background
10. Profit & Loss projections (For ten years)
11. Sensitivity analysis DSCR & IRR
12. Debt services

ANNEXURE-02: Field Surveys (Geodesic)

1. **Topographical survey:** Topographical survey to demarcate the boundaries of the site and block levels at every five-meter distance both ways (to work out the contours).
2. **Borehole data:** Depth up to twice the height of the proposed building or up to solid rock depending upon the height of the building, to analyze the nature of its soil at various levels to work out S.B.C., groundwater levels to arrive at the upthrust. This should be at every five meters, center to center both ways.
3. **Borehole data to tap groundwater:** Depending upon the permission of the authorities concerned, drill boreholes with the help of a water diviner to find out the availability of sufficient groundwater to meet the requirement of the project once when it comes into operation, followed by necessary tests for any treatment required.
4. **Security system:** Employ an experienced security officer who has ample experience managing security staff and is alert to notify the management about any security lapse and take remedial measures.
5. **Water supply for work:** Water supply should be adequate for the project. Explore whether the municipal supply is enough. If not, drill boreholes in the site and test the water sample for its utility. For works whenever authority's permission is required, get the same through proper channels.
6. **Temporary Power:** Work out the total power requirement for the project taking into account all the tools and plants likely to be employed on the project, shift-wise and through the law of averages, i.e., the maximum requirement at the peak period. Apply to the authorities concerned well in advance to avoid delays.

ANNEXURE-03: Costing of 5-Star Hotels or Resorts

Total Development Cost Proforma Template

Architect in some cases, multiple professions

Mechanical Consultant

Electrical Consultant

Plumbing Consultant

Structural Consultant

Civil Consultant Engineer some fees may be paid as part of site survey

Landscape Architect

Interior Designer

Other Consultants (Project Manager, Technical Services cost by Project Coordinator/ Operator, Project Manager, Construction Manager – all staff included).

Subtotal

Transaction Cost

Title & Escrow (Const. Loan): Additional title and escrow fees if site purchased in a separate transaction.

Taxes during construction

Insurance during construction

Appraisal charges: Some lenders may require as-built appraisal as well as site appraisal.

Title & Recording (Permanent Loan) Additional title and escrow fees if the site is purchased in separate transactions.

Tax Credit Application & Reserve Fee

Legal-Construction Loan

Legal-Permanent Loan

Legal-organization

Syndications

Financial Consultant Fees

Accounting & Audit

Builder's Risk Insurance

Sub-Contractor Bonds

Sub Total

Financing Costs

Fee to issuer varies with financing terms

Official Statement printing varies with financing terms

Trustee-Acceptance fee varies with financing terms

Trustee-First Annual fee varies with financing terms

Bond Counsel varies with financing terms

Financial advisor to issuer varies with financing terms

Rating agency varies with financing terms

Under writer's fees and expenses (1.00%) varies with financing terms

Underwriters counsel varies with financing terms

L/C Acceptance fee (0.25%) varies with financing terms

L/C First year's annual fee (1.00%) varies with financing terms

L/C Bank counsel varies with financing terms

Title insurance/closing costs varies with financing terms

Other bank fees (appraisals, etc.) varies with financing terms

Construction interest varies with financing terms

Subtotal

Start-up Costs

Marketing and Advertising

Lease-up reserve based on fill-up and expenses projections

Pre-opening salary and benefits based on staff necessary to open building

Other start-up costs

Subtotal

Total Development Cost

Total Development Cost Proforma Template

Site Acquisition

Market study fees

Site selection fees

Deposit on-site purchase

Balance of site purchase price - purchase price of land

Site survey

Site environmental report conducts environmental investigation required by the lender

Soil testing to determine foundation and building location

Site title search and insurance

Sub Total

Construction Costs

Site Improvements

Clearing, grading, foundation preparation, roads, sidewalks, parking lots, etc. that are outside of building footprint and not landscaping.

On-site utilities - Utility improvements required on building site

Off-site utilities - Utility improvements required to bring utilities to the building site

Landscaping

Building construction costs

Construction contract price including F.F. & E.

Construction contingency - Percentage of construction cost based on the complexity of the project (5-10%).

Sub Total

F.F. & E.

Should include anything necessary to open facility that is not included in construction contract

Furniture common area, office, model room

Outdoor furniture

Office equipment - computer, fax machine, copier, phone system

Kitchen equipment - stove, refrigerators, freezers, dishwasher-may be included in the construction

Kitchen small wares - pots, pans, utensils, dishes, cups, glasses, and flatware

Unit appliances - refrigerator, microwave for resident units – may be included in the construction

Laundry equipment - washers, dryers-may be included in the construction

Laundry supplies - carts, tables, tubs

Linens

Beauty shop equipment may be included in the construction contract

Beauty shop supplies

Maintenance equipment yard tools, repair tools

Housekeeping equipment and supplies - Mops, brooms, vacuum cleaners, extractor

Window treatments may be included in the construction contract

Activities equipment and supplies

Medical equipment and supplies

Subtotal

Municipality Related

These fees will vary significantly by location and are identified through discussions with local officials

Building permits and fees: Building permit/plan check/mechanical/electrical/plumbing, etc.

Planning permits: Design review application/Use permit, environmental review

Planning consultants may be required in complex zoning matters

Water fees - costs paid to the city for fire line, a new meter, water usage fees

Parks - some municipalities assess new developments for park fees

Sewer fees - Costs paid to municipality for hook up to sewer extension lift stations, etc., but distinguished from included costs on and off-site utilities

School fees - some municipalities assess new developments for these fees

Traffic study/impact fees - some municipalities assess new developments for these fees

Other municipal fees

Sub Total

Professional Fees (If not included above)

ANNEXURE-04: Guest Room Items and Cost Analysis

Sl. No.	Item Code	Description of Items	Qty in Nos.	Unit	Rate	Amount	Remarks
		Fixtures & Fittings					
		Bath Tub Area					
1		Bath Tub & Accessories	1	Unit			
2		Tub Faucet (Bath Tub Mixer Incl. Bath Valves	1	Unit			
3		Hand Held Shower Assembly Incl. Diverter & Wall Union	1	Unit			
4		Grab Bar	1	Unit			
5		Double Towel Bar	1	Unit			
6		Shower Drain	1	Unit			
		WC Area					
7		Cascade Wallvit pan	1	Unit			
8		Toilet Paper Holder	1	Unit			
9		Under Counter Wash Basin	1	Unit			
10		Lavatory Faucet (Three Hole Basin Mixer)	1	Unit			
11		Towel Bar	1	Unit			
		Light Fixtures					
12		Wall Sconce entry to Bath/ Wash Basin Area	1	Unit			
13		Wall Sconce Room with diffused Glass Shade (Junction Light, Armoire side)	1	Unit			
14		Floor Lamp Room (Standing Lamp)	1	Unit			
15		Wall Sconce Night Stand (Bed Side)	2	Unit			
16		Desk Lamp	1	Unit			
17		Down Lights Room Window Side and Vestibule Ceiling	2	Unit			
18		Toilet Ceiling Light	2	Unit			
19		Ward Robe Light	1	Unit			
20		Vestibule Ceiling Light	1	Unit			

21		WC Area & Wash Basin Area	2	Unit			
Carpets							
22		Guest Room Carpet	20.7	Sq. Mtr			
23		Carpet Underlays	20.7	Sq. Mtr.			
Grills							
24		Supply Air Grille (0.9 × 0.2)	0.18	Sq. Mtr.			
25		Return Air Grill (Vestibule Area)	0.18	Sq. Mtr.			
26		Toilet Exhaust Grill (0.15 × 0.15)	0.0225	Sq. Mtr.			
Wallpaper							
27		Wall Paper for Guest Room	55	Sq. Mtr.			
28		Wall Paper in Bath Room	3.5	Sq. Mtr.			
Furniture							
29		King Head Board	1	Unit			
30		King Bed Set/Bed Frame	1	Unit			
31		Armoire Large	1	Unit			
32		Night Stand Tall	2	Unit			
33		Night Stand Small	1	Unit			
34		Desk	1	Unit			
35		Side Table	1	Unit			
36		Desk Chair	1	Unit			
37		Lounge Chair	1	Unit			
38		Ottoman	1	Unit			
39		Stool @ Bath	1	Unit			
40		Mirror @ Desk	1	Unit			
41		Television	1	Unit			
42		Mini Electronic Safe	1	Unit			
43		Telephone (Desk @ Bed Side)	2	Unit			
44		Wall Mounted Telephone	1	Unit			
45		Mini Bar	1	Unit			
46		Hair Dryer	1	Unit			
47		Duet Covers, Filling & Lining	1	Unit			
48		King Sham, Filling & Lining	3	Unit			
49		Curtains (Black Out Lining)	2	Unit			
50		Art Work	3	Unit			

51		Door Lock		Unit			
52		Bell	1	Unit			
53		Smoke Detectors/ Response Indicators	1	Unit			
54		Sprinklers		Unit			
55		Peizo Hooter	1	Unit			
1.0 Finishing Works							
56	1.01	Providing & Fixing Gypsum Board Ceiling/ Cornice in Plain/Vertical & Horizontal Surfaces	22.819	Sq. Mtr.			
57	1.02	Fixing Openable Fabric Ceiling Panel in Toilet over Wooden Frame	1.425	Sq. Mtr.			
58	1.03	Providing & Fixing Gypsum Board partition	1	Unit			
59	1.04	Providing P.O.P Punning with P.O.P Gypsum to R.C.C. surfaces on walls & Ceiling	66.056	Sq. Mtr			
60	1.05	Fixing of Wall Covering on Finished P.O.P Punned Surface in Guest Room & Guest Bath	58.5	Sq. Mtr.			
61	1.06	Painting Wall/Ceiling with Plastic Emulsion Paint	41.099	Sq. Mtr.			
2.0 Wood Work							
62	2.01	Providing & Fixing Wood Panelling consisting of Finished Veneer Panels	7.368	Sq. Mtr.			
63	2.02	Providing & fixing Wooden False Ceiling in vestibule Area	4.415	Sq. Mtr.			
64	2.03	Door Frame providing & fixing door frame in solid wood section with rebates, Architrave, etc.	0.0579	Cub. Mtr.			
65	2.04 (a)	Providing & Fixing Main Door Shutter of overall size 2150 mm x 970 mm solid core 50 mm thick with both side veneering in book match style.	1	Unit			
66	2.04 (b)	Sliding Shutters: Providing & Fixing Sliding Door Shutters with one side wood veneering & other side finished mirror panels.		Unit			

67	2.04 (i)	Overall shutter size 2400 mm x 900 mm	1	Unit			
	(ii)	Overall shutter size 2650 mm x 900 mm	1	Unit			
68	2.05	Closet: Providing & Fixing Closet in wood consisting of wall cabinet and luggage Rack	1	Unit			
69	2.06	Skirting: Providing & fixing of skirting in solid wood	24.53	Rn. Mtr.			
70	2.07	Basin Counter: Providing and fixing of stone basin countertop, etc.	1	Unit			
71	2.08	Window Sill: Providing and fixing window sill in solid wood	2.4	Rn. Mtr.			
		3.0 Mirror/Glass Work					
72	3.01	Providing & fixing Plain Mirror Panelling					
	(a)	Bath Tub Wall	1.485	Sq. Mtr.			
	(b)	Wash Basin Counter	1.515	Sq. Mtr.			
73	3.02	Providing & fixing Decorative Glass 10 mm thick frosted behind basin counter	0.276	Sq. Mtr.			
74	3.03	Providing & fixing Decorative Glass partition between WC & Bath area with Granite Ledge	0.651	Sq.Mtr.			
75	3.04	Providing & fixing Plain Glass Shelves on sides of Wash Basin Counter	2	Unit			
76	3.05	Providing & fixing of Oval Shaped Mirror with Stone Shelf	1	Unit			
		4.0 Stone/Granite					
		Work					
77	4.01	Stone Flooring: Providing and Fixing Granite Stone flooring	12.068	Sq.mtr.			
78	4.02	Providing and fixing Granite Stone Skirting	4.505	Sq.Mtr.			
79	4.03	Providing & Fixing Granite Stone Cladding	18.587	Sq.Mtr.			
80	4.04	Extra for Making Openable Access Panel Bath Tub in Marine Grade Ply Backing Clad with Stone	1	Unit			

ANNEXURE-05:
Budget Breakdown for 200 Rooms 5-Star Hotels

(Area of the facility (in sq. mt.) is as the case may be; Estimated Project duration = 24 months)

	Particulars	% of Total cost
A	Land & Acquisition Cost	
01	Land Costs	
	Part -1	
B	Preliminary works/Enabling works such as survey cost & temporary works	0.10%
C	Civil Shell & Core, waterproofing, façade, masonry & plaster & external finishes, etc.	27.00%
D	Interiors- Millwork and Hard Finishes such as floor, ceiling and wall finishes, marble & granite, etc. millwork, doors and windows, glassworks, hardware & acoustics.	20.50%
E	Loose Furniture & Soft Furnishing including fabrics, rugs, carpets, stitching, Artworks & Artifacts & Signages, etc.	4.00%
F	Electrical & Communication low side, Architectural & decorative lighting fixtures, dimmers, façade, external & landscape lighting, switches & sockets, audio & video equipments, CCTV & MATV, High side installations, DG sets & BMS installation, etc.	11.00%
G	Plumbing & Fire Fighting, Plumbing high side & Low side, Sanitary wares and fixtures, General plumbing installations, Firefighting & sprinkler system, Pool filtration & treatments systems, water bodies, LPG Fire extinguishers, HSD fuel oil tanks & STP, etc.	6.00%
H	HVAC Works such as High & Low side.	5.00%
I	Bought-Out Items such as Lifts, FF&E items, Spa& Gym equipment, laundry equipment, Kitchen Equipment, IT equipment, UPS, Telephone System & in-room equipment.	12.00%
J	Landscaping includes Softscape, Hardscape, Gate, Boundary Wall & Paving, etc.	1.54%
K	Operating Supplies	2.25%
L	Architects & Consultancy Fee	5.00%
M	Project Management Cost	5.75%
	Pre-Opening	0.60%
M	Interest	Included
	Total	
	Contingency	Included upto 5.00%
	Grand Total	
	Debt Equity Ratio	As agreed upon

Notes:

1. The estimated cost of 200 Rooms 5-star hotel (excluding land cost) in 2010-2011 in India is around Rs. 125 to 150 crores (with no time and cost escalations). At present, i.e., in 2020, this could be around Rs. 200 crores.
2. The construction time for any 5-star hotel from 200 to 500 rooms in normal times should not exceed 30 months, and the capital invested should be recovered in seven years of operation.
3. If the total cost is x+y+z, then "x" is the land and development cost, "y" is the items shown above and "z" is any unanticipated expenditure cost of delays.
4. In the present day scenario, a super deluxe 5-star hotel would cost around Rs. 1.25 crores/Room (excluding land cost) if the overall number of rooms is 500 or more.

ANNEXURE-06: Suggested Provisions for Amenities, Heights, Clearances and Other Valid Suggestions for Star Hotels

Certain important factors to be kept in mind when it comes to the provision of amenities and space requirements for Luxury Hotels.

1. **Guest Rooms:**
   (*a*) We should have at least one guest floor service area near the service elevator lobby, including linen storeroom, mini bar storage amenity, lockable cabinet, janitor closet, employee toilet, linen shute, linen sorting zone, Ice machines alcove, glasswasher, glass sanitizer. The service elevator lobby should include a trolley parking zone, soiled room, service tray zone, wall-mounted bulletin board, wall-mounted house phone, data outlet for mini bar. The service elevator lobby does not include circulation space in front of the service elevator.

   (*b*) All suites should connect to twin rooms.

   (*c*) 10% to 15% of king rooms to connect to twin rooms.

   (*d*) Each accessible king room to connect to a typical twin room and each accessible twin room to be connected to a typical king room.

   (*e*) Allow for ± 3.30 dimensions from floor to floor at all guest floors.

   (*f*) The king room, the twin room, and standard regency guest room should have at least three fixture bathrooms.

   (*g*) All suites will have at least five fixtures, master bathrooms and walk-in closets.

   (*h*) The general manager's apartment should consist of two bedrooms, a study area, living area, dining area, domestic style kitchen and oversized storage closets.

   (*i*) The club lounge should be located on one of the guest floors, with its entry located just near the guest elevator lobby.

2. **The Food and Beverage Outlets and Reported Support Area:**

   General:

   (*a*) All food and beverage outlets should have ±4.0 meter ceiling height from floor to floor in the public zones.

   (*b*) All food and beverage suite areas (kitchen and pantry) to have a minimum clear ceiling height of 2.85 meters with due consideration for the hood and special kitchen items.

3. **Banqueting and Meeting Facilities:**

   General:

   (*a*) The pre-function room should be located for direct access to each ballroom section.

   (*b*) The ballroom should be divisible into three or more sectors to enable multiple functions.

(*c*) Some meeting rooms may be combined via folding wall systems.

(*d*) Allow for wall systems that adhere to operator standards.

(*e*) Each ballroom section will have a recessed overhead motorized projection screen near the headwall.

(*f*) Ceiling height in the ballroom should have a clear height of 6.5 to 7.0 meters and 3.5 to 4.5 meters in the meeting rooms and board rooms.

(*g*) A-V control room and equipment room should be equally located adjacent to the ballroom.

(*h*) Allow clear ceiling space of 2.85 mt. in the banquet kitchen and dishwashing area and meeting room party for hoods and other special items.

(*i*) The service corridor behind the ballroom and kitchen should have a clear width of 4 meters for multiple sections vestibule for each of the Ball Room Sections.

4. **Additional Public Areas:**

(*a*) Allow double-height (at least 6 meter) for hotel lobby ceiling in public areas.

(*b*) The business centre should be directly connected to hotel guest service centre.

5. **Administrative Office:**

General

(*a*) The front office should be located adjacent to the front desks.

(*b*) The executive office should be located next to the business centre and accessible from the public areas of the hotel lobby and the communication centre.

(*c*) The marketing and sales office, reservation office, the catering and convention offices should be clustered together and easily accessible from the public areas of the lobby. So also the account and information systems offices.

(Local codes should also be taken into account).

5. **Fitness Centre & Spa Facilities:**

General:

(*a*) The fitness centre and spa will cater to the guests and all members of the surrounding community.

(*b*) All spa treatment rooms will be self-contained for all guests and treatments. The service will include the following: pantry, changing areas with full height lockers or wardrobe with wet and dry variety, toilet cubicles, shower, soap, bathtub, treatment area, and outdoor relaxation area.

7. **BOH Support Services:**

General:

(*a*) All F&B stores and fresh areas to have a minimum clear ceiling height of 2.85 meters with consideration for the hood and other special items.

(*b*) Follow operator's flow diagrams for BOH and plant areas and for details of ceiling height etc.

(*c*) For details of the MEP plant room and AHU room, follow the manufacturer's guidelines.

8. **Employee Facilities:**

   General:

   (*a*) Personal training facilities including a language laboratory, training rooms, E-learning centre, and breakfast rooms.

   (*b*) Internet café area should be adjoining the employee café.

   (*c*) Vending and merchandise area should be adjoining employee café.

9. **Parking Facilities:**

   General:

   (*a*) Auto parking facilities should be available for the hotel guests, food & beverage outlet patrons, meeting facilities, guests, spa members.

   (*b*) Outdoor line parking, taxi waiting/parking should be provided at the entrance.

   (*c*) Multiple lanes at the fort cochre should be planned.

ANNEXURE-07: Approximate Cost Details of Hotel Projects Associated by the Author as President/Chief Adviser

Sl. No.	Project Name	Years Construction	Broad details	Total Costs
1	Hotel Centaur Santa Cruz, Bombay	1972-76	Seven Storied Annular Structure - 300 Bed Rooms, 2 Specialty Restaurants, 1 Coffee shop, Banquet Hall, Meeting Rooms, Lobby, Health Club (Total area 30,000 sq.meters).	Rs. 12 Crores (Except Land Cost)
2.	Hotel Yak & Yeti (Phase-1) Kathmandu, Nepal	1975-78	110 Rooms, 2 VVIP Suites, 1 Banquet Hall,1 Coffee Shop, Bar, Reception & Front office, Kitchen & Store.	US$5Million (Except Land cost)
3.	Hotel Yak & Yeti (Phase- II) Kathmandu, Nepal	1990-94	Added 150 rooms including & 8 VIP Suits, 1 Presidential Suite, enlarged Lobby and Shopping Arcade. Added Satellite Kitchen and Addl. Commercial space for casino.	Rs. 60 crores (Nepalese Currency) (Except Land cost)
4.	Grand Hyatt New Delhi	1995-2001	400 Rooms including 1-Presidential Suite, 2-executive Suites and 3-Junior Suites, 2 Specialty Restaurant, 1 Coffee Shop, Lobby, Banquet Hall, and Total built area 55,000 sq.m.	US$80 million (Including cost of the land)
5.	Grand Hyatt Santa Cruz, Bombay	1997-2003	900 Rooms (including 100 Apartments), 3 Restaurants, 1 coffee shop, Total Built Area 1, 10,000 Sq Meters.	Indian Rs. 550 Crores (except Land Cost)
6.	Tarajaon Regency, Kathmandu, Nepal	1994 -98	300 rooms, 6 Suites, Public areas, all put together 25,000 Sq. Meters.	Indian Rs. 200 Crores (Except land cost)
7.	Grand Hyatt New Delhi (Renovation Project	2008-09	Renovation of entire Public Areas and Rooms and Kitchens	Rs. 200 crores.

Note: The costs shown above are based on the information available to the author at the time of construction. If the management had any other overheads, they are also included. Some of the photographs of 5-star hotels undertaken by the author are given on pages: 117 to 119.

ANNEXURE-08: List of Statutory Body Approvals Required Before Starting and Commercial Operations of Hotels

Sl. No.	Name of the Statutory Approval Authority	Purpose of Approval
1	State Electricity Board/Authority/ Corporation	1. Power connection 2. Installation and operation of DG sets
2	State Water Supply & Sewage Board	1. Water supply 2. Sewage connection
3	Pollution Control Board/Committee	For Consent under Air & Water Act
4	Inspector of Lifts/Elevators	For Installation of lifts at the Hotel
5	Local/City Development Authority	1. For Building Completion Certificate 2. Operation of Hotel
6	Central Ground Water Authority	For Registration of Bore Wells/Tubes Well erected by the Company
7	Dept. Of Explosives	Site and Layout of Installations
8	Ministry of Rural Development	Setting up of Cold Rooms
9	Local/City Municipal Corporation	1. License for Boarding House 2. License for Eating House/Restaurants 3. License for Sale of Sweets & Confectionary 4. For Purity of Food, Beverage and Water (under PFA for their hygiene) 5. Sanitation and Water supply
10	State Police Department	1. Hotel, Restaurants & Bar 2. Storage of Gas and other Fuels
11	Reserve Bank of India	Money Changer
12	GST Council	Allotment of GST Number
13	FRRO (Foreign Regional Registration Office)	1. To allow Foreign guests and expatriate employees
14	Other Registrations	1. Labour Laws: PF and ESI 2. Factories Act 3. Excise and Luxury Tax including Bar Licence and the Storage and Bonded Warehouse 4. Weights & Measures (with equipment only)

ANNEXURE-09: Eco Resorts (Ref. Chapter 10)

Eco resorts can be created at suitable places along the Indian coastline starting from Gujarat in the west down to Kerala and then up to West Bengal in the east, i.e., to cover Gujarat, Maharashtra, Goa, Karnataka, Kerala, Tamil Nadu, Andhra Pradesh, Orissa and West Bengal. The resort has to be ecologically sustainable and environment friendly. It could be in clusters to make it economically viable with respect to infrastructure and travel so that each cluster produces revenue not less than USD 1 billion a month, from room tariffs, sale of food, beverage, jewelry, artifacts & handicrafts and income from malls, multiplexes hospitals and sports revenues. Competition between different hotels brands in terms of quality of service naturally increases output.

A. Assumptions:

1. Phase I begins with one cluster in each of the nine states. Phase II starts with one cluster in each of the eight states. Phase III begins with one cluster in each of the eight states (Goa in Phase I only).
2. Each cluster to have 25 numbers of 5-star resorts and 25 numbers of 3-star resorts. Each resort to have 500 rooms on average and a total of 25,000 Rooms.
3. Land required for each 5-star resort is an average of 25 acres, and for 3-star resorts,10 acres. Total land required is 875 acres. The actual area of the resort can vary substantially between one another depending on overall planning.
4. The acreage for each cluster is 1875 to 2000 acres, including 625 acres for infrastructure (875 acres for Resorts, 375 acres for highway and 625 acres for infrastructure).
5. The length of the entire resort facing the sea is 25 km.
6. The connecting highway to all resorts (8 Main lanes + 2 service lanes) is 200 feet wide. This also serves as a landing strip for Dornier or Fokker aircraft by providing a landing strip parallel to the highway at a suitable point. Infrastructural facilities to be on the land side of the road.
7. Highway in the resort area connects to the nearest National/State highway.

The total infrastructure area excluding highway works out to almost 625 acres for each cluster.

B. The infrastructure to be provided for each cluster could be as follows:

1. Cluster may need a beach length of 25 km.
2. If the sea is rough, "spurs" have to be provided.
3. The resort is to be provided with water and electricity at one point. Available solar power options should be adequately utilized.
4. Adequate drainage and sewage systems to be provided, including sewage and water treatment plants for each cluster, with provisions for recycling the treated sewage water for arboriculture.

5. If any, the surrounding villages to be spruced up with clean roads and sanitation and could have some auditoria for local cultural shows.
6. Staff quarters for 28,000 staff men, ten 100-bed hospitals for each cluster and a police station plus coast guard office. The office of the R.D.A (Resort Development Authority) - one window for all the matters of the resort owner vs. government, to be on the opposite side of the highway (not on the same side of the resort). The infrastructure facility is to be built as hotel work starts so that the staff accommodation is ready at least six months before commissioning. The staff accommodation could be storied blocks with one to five bay apartments. The hospital could be suitably located, should be able to serve the guests and the staff. The R.D.A should provide power and water supply. The staff colony and the Hospital are to be built and maintained by private agencies on B.O.T. basis and regulated by the R.D.A. with a covenant. The wood carving, leather craft, batik silk, etc., with premium handbags (handcrafted), hoes and other knick-knacks, could have a suitable area on the infrastructure side. The other infrastructure on B.O.T. basis is multiplex + mall (10 Nos.) + 3 stadiums for 10 football grounds + 10 hockey grounds + 10 basketball and volleyball grounds and 100,000 sq.ft. greenhouse + 200 mercedes buses + 10 Fokker or Dornier aircraft + 1 helicopter + one ATC tower for controlling air traffic.
7. The R.D.A has to enter into a covenant with the hoteliers to recover the cost of land, water and electricity arrangements excluding solar from the resorts on a 20 years recovery basis with 5% simple interest expected to be around Rs. 2875 crore for each cluster.
8. The RDA can decide if the staff accommodation and amenities could be the investor's responsibility.

C. Cost Estimates:

1. The cluster has 12500 5-star rooms and 12500 3-star rooms.
2. A 5-star room in 2021-22 could vary in cost from Rs. 1.25 crore to Rs. 1.75 crore per room, i.e., an average of crore Rs. 1.5 crore per room.

   Therefore, 12,500 5-star rooms may cost on an average 12,500 × Rs. 1.5 crore = Rs. 18750 crore ...(1)
3. Three star rooms may cost Rs. 0.4 crore to Rs. 0.5 crore per room.

   Therefore, 12,500 3-star rooms may cost 12,500 × Rs. 0.5 crore = Rs. 6250 crores ...(2)
4. Total cost of 25,000 rooms = Rs .25, 000 crore. [US $ 3.3 billion]
5. Basic infrastructure, i.e., water, electricity, drainage and seafront, air strip and highway, can cost Rs. 2500 crore.
6. This will be the cost charged to the investor towards land cost on a 20-year payment basis with 5% interest.
7. Total investment for cluster = Rs. 25000 crore + Rs. 2500 crore = Rs. 27500 crore or US$3.660 billion. [@ Rs. 75 = $1]
8. BOT infrastructure cost per cluster is estimated at Rs. 6250 crore. This is 25% of Rs. 25000 crores of the investor's components.

9. The cost per cluster in Phase II may increase by 5% and Phase III by 10%. Hence, the cost in Phase II = US$ 3.666 billion × 1.05 = US$ 3.85 billion.

   the cost in the Phase III = US$ 3.666 billion × 1.10 = US$ 4.36 billion.

   Average of all three phases = US$ 3.84 billion.

   So, the average cost of a cluster + basic infrastructure comes to US$ 4.330 billion.

   Therefore 25 clusters + basic infrastructure = US$ 103 billion.
10. The investment for 25 clusters without BOT infrastructure = US$103 billion.
11. BOT infrastructure per cluster = US$ 6280 billion for I Phase.

    Add 5% and 10%, respectively, for Phase II and III.

    The average cost of BOT infrastructure for all three phases comes to US$ 6650 billion.
12. Total BOT infrastructure for 25 clusters = 25 × Rs. 6600 crore = Rs. 16,500 crore or US$ 22 billion.

In other words, by treating the BOT infrastructure independent of the cost of the clusters, we are helping the investors save almost 20% of investment by means of BOT.

Tsunami and Cyclone Precautions for the Resorts

1. It is usual practice to keep BOH and plant areas out of public view. Generally in cities, these are located in basements to control noise, fumes, etc., from affecting the guests. In the present case, these could be nearer to the entry point, with the underground plant room on the ground floor and kitchen, laundry and BOH areas on the first floor. The whole facility is surrounded by RCC retaining wall with sloped earth fill around and suitable landscaping. As these services are generally high roofed, the total height of both floors will be nearly 25 ft. This height is safe from average Tsunami wave heights. So, the public areas such as lobby lounge reception, front office, business centre, shopping arcade, banquet halls, pre-function halls, meeting rooms including speciality restaurants, restrooms can come on top of the utility and BOH areas. As an emergency measure, the guests can gather in these areas on such occasions.
2. All the cables and service connections should be underground.
3. The buildings should preferably be system-built in RMC concrete using "Mivan" or similar monolithic systems where walls are cast along the floor and roof slab with all conduits and pipe inserts in place. No plaster is needed on the concrete surfaces, and the painting can be done directly on the finished concrete surface. The doors and windows are jammed into place, and sewage sullage pipes are embedded in the wall with dents already created in the forms. The terrace structure, if any, could be pitched RCC slabs on columns with roof tiles embedded on top. In the event of a cyclone or tsunami, the doors and windows could be covered with pre-fabricated covers, which will be plugged into the doors and windows. The room blocks could also be built with "Mivan" or similar system forms where the floors and roofs are cast with the walls. A wireless tsunami warning system has to be established along with the monitoring process.
4. In the event of a cyclone, a fully protected underground shelter in buildings will house the people.
5. The walls facing the sea could be circular, adequately strengthened for shear.

ANNEXURE-10: Infrastructure Details of a Resort Zone

SEA	RESORT ZONE 25 KM	6-LANE HIGHWAY	INFRASTRUCTURE ZONE	Infrastructure Details
S E A	R E S O R T Z O N E 25 KM	6- L A N E H I G H W A Y	I N F R A S T R U C T U R E Z O N E	Infrastructure Details: 1. Chargeable to investor for each Hotel/Resort: (a) Highway (6-lane) connecting the Cluster and Control tower at one end. (b) Improvements in the seashore. (c) Water supply installations (one point). (d) Electricity Installations (one point). (e) Chargeable for each Resort = 2% for the cost for the Cluster. (f) Water and Electricity charges on consumption. 2. B-O-T basis: (a) Residential accommodation for the staff employed in the resorts. (b) 2 × 500 bed Hospital for the whole cluster. (c) Sports facilities: Golf grounds at least 4,9 hole Golf course for each cluster. Football Stadiums 2/Cluster. Hockey Stadiums 2/Cluster. Volleyball, Badminton, Basket Ball stadiums 4/Cluster. (d) Multiplexes/Malls 6/Cluster. (e) Green Houses 2(1,00,000 sq.ft. each) (f) Mercedus buses- 50 for each cluster. (g) Dornier or Fokker Aircraft – 10 for each cluster. (h) One Helicopter(10-seater) for each cluster. (i) Infrastructure area excluding the highway is 625 acres and includes internal roads. (j) Infrastructure spread could vary depending on topography. Width of 6-lane highway = 50 meters. Width of Infrastructure zone = 90 meters.

ANNEXURE-11: Abbreviations Used in the Book

A H U	Air Handling Unit
A M D	Annual Maintenance Department
B O H	Back of House
B O Q	Bill of Quantities
B O T	Build, Operate and Transfer
D G Set	Diesel Generating Set
D S C R	Debt Service Coverage Rate
ECGC	Export Credit Guarantee Corporation
ECGS	Export Credit Guarantee System
F & B	Food & Beverage
F F & E	Furniture, Fittings and Equipment
F P	Fire Protection
HT	High Tension
H V A C	Heating, Ventilation and Air-Conditioning
I D	Interior Designer
I R R	Internal Rate of Return
L/C	Letter of Credit
LT	Low Tension
M E P	Mechanical, Electrical and Plumbing Engineering
N I T	Notice Inviting Tenders
P & I	Protection & Indemnity
P A	Principal Architect
P O P	Plaster of paris
R C C	Reinforced Cement Concrete
R D A	Resort Development Authority
S B C	Safe Bearing Capacity
S T P	Sewage Treatment Plant
U P S	Uninterrupted Power Supply
W C	Water closet

THE AUTHOR'S PORTFOLIO
SELECTED PROJECTS BY THE AUTHOR

Grand Hyatt, New Delhi
View from Pool Side

Grand Hyatt, New Delhi
Banquet Hall

Hyatt Regency, New Delhi
Display Kitchen

Hyatt Regency, Kolkata
Banquet Hall

Hyatt Regency, Kolkata
Banquet Hall

Grand Hyatt, Mumbai

Grand Hyatt, Mumbai
Bar

Hyatt Regency, Kathmandu

Hyatt Regency, Kathmandu
Twin Rooms

Hyatt Regency, Kathmandu
Lounge

Hotel Yak & Yeti, Kathmandu
(Both the phases)

Hotel Yak & Yeti, Kathmandu
Restaurant

Hotel Yak & Yeti, Kathmandu
Interior View

Hotel Yak & Yeti, Kathmandu
Banquet Hall